WILD WEST

Village

NOT A MEMOIR

(Unless I Win an Oscar, Die Tragically, or Score a Country #1)

LOLA KIRKE

Simon & Schuster

New York Amsterdam/Antwerp London Toronto Sydney New Delhi

Simon & Schuster
1230 Avenue of the Americas
New York, NY 10020

First Simon & Schuster hardcover edition January 2025

SIMON & SCHUSTER and colophon are registered
trademarks of Simon & Schuster, LLC

For information about special discounts for bulk purchases,
please contact Simon & Schuster Special Sales at 1-866-506-1949
or business@simonandschuster.com.

The Simon & Schuster Speakers Bureau can bring authors to
your live event. For more information or to book an event, contact the
Simon & Schuster Speakers Bureau at 1-866-248-3049 or visit
our website at www.simonspeakers.com.

Interior design by Joy O'Meara

Manufactured in the United States of America

1   3   5   7   9   10   8   6   4   2

Library of Congress Cataloging-in-Publication Data is available on file.

ISBN 978-1-6680-3557-3
ISBN 978-1-6680-3559-7 (ebook)

For my family,
who shaped my character and
made room for many others in my life.

Also, for Austin. I started writing for you.
When you told me to keep going, I found me.

AUTHOR'S NOTE

With this book, I tell a lot of complicated stories. I don't, however, offer a complete one. There are swaths of things I have not articulated. Some because I can't—they are not mine to. Others because I don't know how to. While it is easy for me to muse about more complicated dynamics, understanding simplicity is much harder. I don't have adequate language for the sound of my mother's laugh in concert with mine or the safety I felt in my father's arms. The sovereignty of being on my big brother's shoulders or other moments I thought would never end, like Irma Thomas singing softly to my sisters and me over the car stereo, lulling us to sleep, mouths harmoniously agape, on night drives home. I am much more practiced at finding lightness in darkness. This is a book about identity forged in fire. Like a flare, I hope it reaches you, perhaps even illuminating flames you yourself walked through, to sometimes glimpse the warm glow of being alive.

INTRODUCTION

When I first told my mother that not only Simon but *also Schuster* wanted to publish my book, she made the word "yay" sound like a deflating balloon before asking:

"Wait—aren't you a bit *young* to be writing a *memoir?*"

Though my mother has admittedly started fudging my age to make herself sound younger, I am confident she really does know it. Ignoring her question, I feverishly attempted to explain that my book wasn't exactly a *memoir* but a collection of personal essay–type stories about family dynamics—ours, specifically—and also about womanhood, Hollywood, country music, class, and, of course, New York City. I marveled at how intelligent I sounded, confident she'd feel the same and say so.

"That's interesting," she said instead, like it wasn't.

By the time we hung up, I couldn't help but agree. It wasn't interesting. Who cared what I had to say? Sure, I'd enjoyed some success as an actress (the thief with a cold sore

1

in *Gone Girl*, Greta Gerwig's foil in *Mistress America*, and a hardworking, harder-partying oboist in Amazon's *Mozart in the Jungle*). I'd even been on magazine covers and up for some awards. But they weren't big ones, like *Vogue* or a Nobel Peace Prize. Not even the few (fairly) well-received country albums I'd released could help me. I was a nobody, a great shortcoming when you have spent your life on track to be a *somebody*. I was ordinary—until I remembered something extraordinary: I had been raised by wolves. In the wilderness. And I had survived.

To be clear, these were beautiful, rich, artistic wolves who repurposed vintage nightgowns as party dresses, and the wilderness I'm speaking of consisted of various brownstones scattered below Fourteenth Street, where my family relocated from London when I was four. After all, we couldn't just move to New York, a city many people can only dream of visiting. We had to move to *the Village*—a historic neighborhood synonymous with the bohemian and the beautiful.

I suppose this suited us. My father was a rock star and a founding member of the seminal British bands Free and Bad Company. My mother was a one-of-a-kind interior decorator and clothing designer. For years, she owned the legendary Perry Street boutique Geminola, its name a whimsical combination of my siblings' and mine. For my oldest sister, Domino, there was the "mino." For my middle sister, Jemima, "emi." As for me, little baby Lola, a whole "ola." Meanwhile, Greg, the only boy, whose normal name and unibrow could be clearly traced to my mother's first marriage, received a small but pivotal "G."*

Early on, my parents nurtured the four of us into distinct creative roles based on our childhood interests. It was sort of like *The Royal Tenenbaums*, except no one was any good at tennis and our house was nicer. I was on deck to be the family movie star (every affluent family of Anglo New Yorkers has at least *one!*); Jemima, the next Picasso; Domino, a world-renowned singer; and Greg, a groundbreaking street photographer. But since artists are known for rebelling as much as they are for seeking parental approval, inevitably, we shook things up a bit and tore off our neat artistic paths. Eventually, I took a break from treading the boards to explore playing guitar and writing prose on this very sauce-covered laptop. Jemima, meanwhile, became an actress, starring in HBO's *Girls*, among other credits; Domino, a sought-after doula *and* singer; and Greg, a part-time inventor, full-time father, and commercial photographer.

Not only were we raised by artists to be artists; we also spent much of our youth surrounded by them. David Bowie turned down my sister's offer to use her hands as an ashtray at one of our legendary Christmas parties—*where the Shirelles were performing*. Courtney Love both flooded and set

---

* After this introduction, my siblings will be referred to only as their Geminola pseudonyms: G for Greg, Mino for Domino, Emi for Jemima. I, on the other hand, will remain Lola, as this is my book and I absolutely do not want to be known as Ola. ☺

fire to our sprawling home during her prolonged stay there. When Liv Tyler wasn't filming installments of *The Lord of the Rings*, she babysat me. Did I just drop something? Yes, a bunch of names. Sorry! The housekeeper's coming by later to pick them up! But don't let the fresh-cut flowers and the framed Longos fool you. My family is still rather wolfish. We move fast and travel far in search of food.* We are exceptionally good-looking. And some of us aren't exactly who you'd want to come across alone at night by the light of a full moon. Because some of us can be quite fierce.

Eager as I was to run with our pack, I often craved a safer kind of love, declared at a lower volume and not just after screaming matches. Out with my mother's gold Mercedes convertible! In with a family minivan! Out with the brownstone that so closely resembled an expensive French brothel! In with a white picket fence and two-car garage!

Don't get me wrong: there were many perks to my upbringing. I have seen the Rolling Stones about a hundred times for free and from side stage. For years, I felt absolutely zero shame about public meltdowns (the world was our therapist's waiting room!). But growing up as I did had its less savory elements. Like learning about siblings I'd never met, in places I was equally unaware of (what was this "Arizona"?). Spending spring break visiting family in rehab. The constant feeling of having too much, never being enough, and still wanting more.

---

* US Fish and Wildlife Service.

Professional success, it seemed, was the only remedy for the profound feelings of personal failure I perceived around me. Having spent my life feeling Important Adjacent—which sounds kind of like the name a realtor gives an up-and-coming neighborhood to make it more enticing to buyers, but really means you're valuable only because you're near something else that is—I looked forward to a future in which I was considered important myself. Only then, I believed, would my family listen to me. Only then would they see: it made *no* sense to favor cool-looking broken antique kitchen appliances instead of functional new ones. And it certainly made no sense to be so unhappy all the time.

When I first set out to write this book, I didn't plan on going into any of that. Initially, in fact, I envisioned the whole thing as a slightly better version of being stuck next to me at a dinner party: I'd talk endlessly about myself but spill my martini on the page instead of all over you, with the added bonus that in the morning, *I wouldn't have to worry that I'd admitted I still don't know where my vulva is!* Because my editor would just delete that part! (. . . Right? . . . Carina? You'll delete that part?) But writing has helped me focus the blurry lens of my privilege and pain. Now I see how to create from that place instead of destruct from it. I also see how underneath all the extraordinary elements I might write about lies one *very* ordinary desire: to feel loved. Feeling like you aren't can drive you crazy. Seeing the ways in which you are can be difficult, especially when the kind of love you know can be as loud, lonely-making, and life-affirming as New York City itself.

I do appreciate my mom's ambivalence about my writing this book—I mean, *really*, what parent wants to read about their daughter sitting idle at a threesome? Especially when said daughter was raised to believe in the value of hard work! Other family members have voiced their anxiety too, and I understand their fear. Becoming a character in someone else's story is bewildering—all the more so when you are still writing your own. (And I do mean that literally, as pretty much everyone in my family welcomed the news of my book by telling me about one of theirs they have in the works.)

But the truth is, what you're reading isn't a tell-all. Nor is it, as my sister Jemima believes, a biography of her. Nor is it either an indictment of my parents' missteps—though I mention quite a few, as they make for good stories and are crucial for character development. It isn't even a memoir—unless I actually *do* win an Oscar, die tragically between now and the time of print, or write a couple country #1s. It's a map I drew of how I navigated the larger-than-life personalities I grew up around, oriented toward the true north of my own identity. It winds through Hollywood.

Weaves through Nashville. Accidentally routes through *Gainesville*, where I went once because I got confused! Complete disaster! May it be useful to you as you blaze your own trail. Now let's go! We've got a lot of ground to cover.*

---

* Unstable as it is, I suggest you wear heels. Or colorful cowboy boots. I wouldn't want you to feel underdressed, and I loathe a sensible shoe.

PART ONE

Farm Camp, Fat Replicas, and a Family Vacation to Rehab

If you want to know what God thinks of money, just look at the people he gave it to.

—Dorothy Parker

THE CURSE

On the cover of the workbook, there's a cartoon drawing of a daisy with eyes, smiling at her reflection in a mirror she's holding in her little white-gloved hands. I joke to the group that I'm gonna get the image as a back tat. Precisely one person thinks this is funny. The rest carry on with the serious business of finding the page with the friendly looking tree.

Even though I am thirty-three and essentially perfect, I often still feel the same messy pain I did when I was a kid. According to the self-help group I've recently started attending, this is because I am an "adult child," i.e., I respond to many adult situations the way a child might. When you grow up fast, as I did in New York City, I think, you never really grow up. For a moment this makes me feel very cool. I picture myself wearing a beret tilted just so, exhaling smoke from a candy cigarette, because I'm trying to quit. Then I recall a magnet I used to look at on my old math tutor's fridge:

PUT THE FUN BACK IN DYSFUNCTIONAL!

When I was a kid, this sentiment made me feel seen: *My family puts the fun back in dysfunctional!* I'd think proudly each time I saw it. Then I'd ask my tutor to do the rest of my homework so I could lie down. But now that one of my sisters doesn't talk to my mom, my mom doesn't talk to my dad, my dad believes my mom tried to have him *killed*, and our collective love language seems to be talking shit about each other, I'm not so sure how fun our dysfunction really is.

Fill in the tree below with the names of your family members and their corresponding addictions! the tree barks. So I do. Once I begin, I am surprised at how little I really know.

Mom's side: well, her sister died of a heroin overdose . . . so that. Then there was the gambler. Lots of shopping. Etc. . . . I can just about complete it through my maternal great-grandparents when I realize I have no idea what their names were or what, if anything, they were addicted to. Since they were Jewish, I'm going to assume they didn't drink much (most of the ones I know don't—sensitive stomachs). And since they lived in olden times, I'm going to further assume their lives were somewhat war-torn and fully sepia. They had four kids. They worshipped. They left Baghdad for Manchester. But with them, they brought *the curse.*

My dad has told me about "the curse" of my mother's side several times. This is likely because he can't remember having told me about it before. Because imagine a goldfish. Now imagine a rock star railing cocaine off a pair of perky '70s tits. Put those things together inside an older man in a soft cashmere sweater, and there you have my father. Make no mistake, I have long benefited from the gaps in his memory. I can dependably impress him simply by repeating old achievements. Still, it is a bit of a drag to hear over and over about how all the women in my family are cursed.

Legend has it—

Fuck. Honestly, I can't really remember either.

Let's position this narrative outside a large multicolored tent, at the foot of the Zagros Mountains (no idea if my family was even from around there, but when you google "mountain range iraq," that's what comes up. The area looks gorgeous, though!). Camels abound. A lone woman cooks an aromatic stew on an open fire. A moon thin as God's . . . thumbnail . . . lights the night sky. Stars wink. The young woman is excited. They are celebrating something. For the occasion, she has donned her brightest skirt. Lined her eyes with her blackest kohl. Beaten the rugs. Slaughtered the goats. Done this all in the quickest of hurries, lest her husband return before she is ready and find out her secret: that she is a human being with other shit to do besides dote on him.

The moon is getting higher in the sky now, and she has completed all her tasks. She sits pretty and stirs the pot. And waits. And . . . waits. And still he doesn't come. Eventually, the wood is all burned up. The stew has grown cold. The woman is assuming the worst when she hears a moan in the distance. She slips into her little pointed slippers to slide across the sand and investigate. The moans grow louder. Thunder cracks in the sky, when a burst of lightning reveals a fate worse than death: her husband is fucking her sister. In that moment, her heart shrivels up into a bitter little raisin. And that bitter little raisin heart is what got passed down to all her female descendants, including yours truly!

. . . And give or take a few details, according to my dad's "memory" and my creative license, that's the curse: the women on my mom's side of the family are doomed to be bitter and angry, while the men, as far as I can tell, are doomed to be completely fine, just bald. While this sucks for us gals, I like to think the joke's really on them. With every year that their hairlines recede, I grow *more hair*! And in places I never thought possible, like my chin, neck, nipples, and in coarse black patches on the backs of my thighs.

In truth, I have been hairy since day one. With a shock of tall black hair and many chins that spilleth over, I was born looking like I'd left my husband of thirty years for a woman named Pat, then started collecting reptiles.

"Let's hope she's intelligent," my grandmother said upon first seeing me, her accent like acid flowing from a perfect mouth. With her Hitchcock-blond looks, she had an icy beauty, which she successfully passed down to subsequent generations. Successfully, it seemed, until me.

"She will have great character," she concluded.

Of course, I never actually heard my grandmother say any of this because I was an infant. I just know that she did because my mom told me *all the time*. You see, beauty was *very* important in my family. For as long as I can remember, I have been surrounded by it. Our dogs, willowy golden retrievers, were beautiful. Our English gardens, lush with tulips and benevolent foxes, were beautiful. My parents seemingly had no ugly friends. It would be easy to mistake our early family photo albums for a coffee-table book on London's answer to Studio 54: everyone was just as glamorous, and I'm certain there were as many drugs. Photos of beach vacations show my mother and her brigade of ever-topless friends, diet-pill-thin and laughing. Cigarettes burn in their mouths while their children burn in the background.

Turn the page and . . .

Oh, God no, go back! Actually, don't. Stay. *What*—I mean—*who* is that?

Well, it's me, smiling cross-eyed.

Okay. Got it. But what is *it*—I mean *are you*—wearing?

Well, it's a onesie, silly. Patterned with cats who are reading books, to telegraph my intelligence, because what, may I ask, could be more intelligent *than cats reading books*?

Ah, okay, gotcha, great. Turn the page again and—

HOLY SHIT! WHY ARE THERE SO MANY PHOTOS OF THIS?

Suddenly, the album has transformed. You are no longer behind the scenes of a fun '80s remake of *La Piscine*. You are now touring the studio that brought you *Dinosaurs*. The annotations cease to be sexy, funny comments about nearby celebrities or how great someone's butt is. They are literal, straightforward.

"Lola laughing," one reads, under a picture of—you guessed it—me laughing, with the haircut of a squat, forgotten member of Spinal Tap.

"Lola getting ready for a nap," reads another. And wouldn't ya know? I am lying down.

Same haircut—think man with bangs.

"Lola looking at something," reads the caption to another snap of me, staring cross-eyed, drool pooling into the folds of my chins.

It's not just the photos that are less alluring than their precedents. The handwriting captioning the photos is different too. Unlike my mother's spunky script, it's bubbly and belabored. Like me. Because it's *my* handwriting. I added my own photos to the family album. Attempting to fit in to their glamorous and cool narrative, I crowbarred myself into it, achieving the reverse effect and standing out even more.

This theme started early. After an accident with scissors when I was four—turns out you cannot cut your hair *longer*—I received a scarring emergency pixie cut, which set me back from my goal about thirty inches. Far from looking like my beautiful big sisters, as intended, I now looked like a stand-in for a young Brad Renfro.

Shortly after, we moved from London to New York City. Immediately, things were off to a rough start. First, our suitcases were stolen out of the back of our taxi from the airport, leaving us with no choice but to outfit ourselves in the decidedly basic Gap. But it wasn't until we turned the key in the door of our newly rented apartment that things got truly frightening.

She was above the fireplace. Naked, with legs cut off at the knee and bleeding. The hair at her groin was full and undulating, like a nest of snakes. Her eyes were red and pleading. My mother and sisters tried to explain that she was only a painting. She wasn't real. But this made no sense to me. A child, I still believed art was just supposed to be pretty. *She* was ugly. Confrontational. Suffering. I avoided the room entirely until one day when my mother laid a bedsheet out on the living room floor, encouraging my sisters and me to decorate it however we wanted. In black Sharpie, we drew flowers and fairies with wings and wands. A castle in the distance. Shortly after, the sheet was draped over the canvas. The room became my favorite in the house.

In that moment, my mother taught me the sacred art of transforming a woman's pain into beauty. It was a journey she was well versed in. With a bold lick of paint or an antique piano shawl, charmless rentals were made inviting. With a team of non-English-speaking builders she fought like torrid lovers, the possibilities were endless. While her gift for visually creating the world she'd rather inhabit had its complications, it has always been inspiring to me, even in my youth. With my awful haircut, I was tired of being confused for a little boy. I decided to take matters into my own hands.

"I want a wig," I barked at Rose, my beloved Welsh

nanny who'd moved to the States with us. We slept in mismatched twin beds in our shared room.

"A *wig*?" she balked in her Welsh brogue.

Confusing her incredulity for jealousy, I offered to get her one too. Politely, she declined.

When Rose arrived to pick me up from kindergarten that afternoon, she pulled a neat red bob out of a plastic Patricia Field bag. Placing it atop my head, I demanded that from here on out, whenever I donned my wig, Rose refer to me only as "Anna." Anna was everything I was beginning to feel I wasn't. Anna's family was normal. Anna belonged. Anna was beautiful.

On the bus ride home, Anna fell asleep on Rose's shoulder. Bouncing south of Fourteenth Street, I awoke to discover my Anna wig had slumped off to the side, revealing my short Lola hair underneath. Fellow travelers looked on in confusion and pity. Perhaps they already knew what I had yet to learn: transforming pain into beauty is no small feat.

These days, if I see a person muttering to themselves in a wig on a city bus, I try to see them only as they wish to be. Marilyn Monroe or at least her pretty cousin. I look away before I perceive the little girl underneath, trembling under the weight of a woman she imagines more valuable.

I THINK I CAN

When we were growing up, my sister Emi, almost six years my senior, was everything to me. Conversely, I was nothing to her. While this dynamic undoubtedly scarred me emotionally, it also left literal marks. When I was three and we still lived in London, she encouraged me with unprecedented kindness to jump from our jungle gym into her arms. No offer had ever been more enticing.

"Promise to catch me?" I negotiated, preparing to take the leap.

"Promise." She smiled, opening her arms wide. I closed my eyes as she counted down from three. On one, I jumped. Her laugh receded into the distance. I hit the ground with a thud. She had run away. To this day, I bear the mark under my chin. Allegedly, this is the most common place for children to have scars, which makes me feel less alone. Perhaps I wasn't the only little girl to fall prey to a merciless big sister. Though I imagine few were as merciless as she was.

At a friend's pool the following summer, Emi stole my swimsuit off my body under the water. Then she flushed it down the toilet. As I wept, naked and ashamed, our brother, G, retaliated by giving her a "swirlie," i.e., flushing her head in the toilet. On the car ride home, her face was so red with embarrassment that I felt bad. I reached my hand across the seat toward her. To my surprise, she took it.

When Emi passed double digits, subtle shades of love began to sprout from her usual animosity. On a Caribbean Christmas vacation one year, I emerged from the ocean with a painful jellyfish sting. Elated, she pissed on me.

"It's the only way!" she cried gleefully.

The following spring, I was running a game of Wiffle ball into the ground, having had the fair share of additional strikes allotted to youngest children. As my teammates began to yawn, dreaming of hot dogs and Slip 'N Slides, Emi, who was playing shortstop for our opponents, charged in my direction.

"Just. Say. 'I think I can,'" she whispered into my ear, her English accent making her sound like a smart Victorian ghost. "When the ball is coming closer, you repeat it, over and over. Like this: 'I think I can, I think I can, I think I can.'"

I looked at her, confused.

"If you think you can do it, you can do it," she clarified before running back to her position in the field. I didn't hit the ball, but they let me run bases anyway. Her trick worked for something.

Emi's tenderness was like a secret only I knew. To everyone else, she was still a pest. Or maybe a tyrant, in that she was full of power and not so easily squashed. Her fights with our mother were one of the central storylines of our family drama, in which we were all innocent bystanders and she was the city's most ruthless villain. Battles erupted in toy stores, in restaurants, on airplanes. Anywhere. Everywhere.

"She's so unpleasant," our mother would sigh aloud in the aftermath. While I saw her point, I had a hard time agreeing. Sure, Emi took great pains to publicly humiliate me. But sometimes, when no one was looking, she'd trace gentle circles on my back. They sent tingles up my spine and left me feeling for a moment like we were floating atop a calm, warm sea. Very pleasant indeed.

Still, Emi mostly avoided me at all costs. Except when she needed a subject for her art.

"Look dead," she instructed as she straddled me with her camera one afternoon around the time I was nine. We were in a graveyard out on Long Island, the big one between our summer house and town. Usually, I held my breath while passing it, to avoid possession, then said "jackrabbit" a thousand times to be extra sure. For Emi, however, I would do anything, including lie against a dead child's tombstone from the 1800s, carefully made up in red lipstick she'd applied to me herself. I liked when she did my makeup. It meant we had to be close.

"You're breathing too much."

"It's hard not to," I complained.

"SHHH!" She snapped the Polaroid, shaking it with professional confidence as it developed. "Your eyes are open!" she scolded once it did, before insisting I lie back down so we could try again.

Despite how much she proclaimed to dislike me, I remained Emi's most frequent subject. During one particular sitting, she asked me to pose only in my underwear, holding a cigarette.

"But I'm only ten, don't you think—"

"You don't have to smoke it."

I perched myself anxiously at the foot of her bed, a Marlboro Medium fuming between my fingers. The smoke kept getting in my eyes.

IthinkIcanIthinkIcanIthinkIcan, I repeated to myself silently, determined not to give up.

She smiled coldly at me for a second—the warmest I'd ever seen her. But as her eyes darted between the canvas, my face, and my body, a peaceful feeling settled over me. Feeling seen, I no longer needed to be heard. My thirst for a more usual sisterly arrangement was satisfied by the novel relationship blossoming between us: that of artist and her muse.

The naked ten-year-old smoking version of me hung framed in gold in our foyer for about a decade, until we moved. It wasn't the kind of portrait I typically saw in my friends' family homes. Though, of course, we weren't typical. Our home was part house, part museum, curated expertly by my mother. It was a bit dysfunctional. Highly unconventional. But it was by far the most beautiful.

HUNGRY GHOST

In hindsight, my yearning for normalcy—or at least my version of it—was evident in the variety of games I played as a child. All through elementary school, I was either an unspecified businesswoman in love with her boss and his son (my friend Tilly down the street played both), or a sort of simple country wife. While the former game involved a lot of dry humping, the latter required only that I tie my baby blanket around my waist like an apron and do things like tuck stuffed animals into makeshift beds. I was just pulling a freshly baked pie out of a drawer one evening when my eldest sister, Mino, came home from celebrating her thirteenth birthday. Since women in our family didn't get bat mitzvahed (only the boys got the male equivalent because we were "real Jews," a fact I found confusing, as we never went to synagogue), my mother had arranged for Mino to undergo an alternate rite of passage: a tattoo. Stretching the neck of her T-shirt, Mino revealed an angry, bleeding drawing of her namesake, a domino, on her right shoulder. I marveled at her sophistication.

Soon after, Mino was enrolled at a legendary high school in Midtown with a performing arts focus. There, she'd hone her craft as a singer while also undergoing an identity crisis. To better fit in among her peers in the New York City school system, Mino obscured her posh West London roots with gold nameplate earrings, a puffer jacket, and lip liner at least six shades darker than her lipstick.

"You speak Spanish, right?" she asked our multilingual mother as they mounted the school steps one afternoon, for parent teacher conferences.

"No!" my mother guffawed in her staunchly British accent. Mino lowered her head in sadness.

When one of her favorite rappers died that winter, Mino too was dead to the world, locking herself in her bedroom for days. I sat vigil in the hallway, playing an assortment of sex games with Barbies, while Rose left plates of food outside her door.

A few months passed, but Mino's sadness remained. Her rebellion grew alongside it. Night after night, she would sneak out. Night after night, she would also be caught sneaking out and get grounded. Then she'd do it again. *That's* how good clubs were back then.

When I learned Tilly's father managed another one of Mino's favorite artists—an R&B singer who was fortunately still among us—I implored him to get us tickets to her concert at Radio City. Since I was moderately charming and he wasn't aware that his daughter and I spent most of our playdates unknowingly enacting the plots of bad pornos, he obliged. Mino squealed with delight when I told her of my victory. I felt confident she'd never leave my side again.

The night of, the two of us were waiting for a cab on a street corner, jumping up and down with cold and excitement, when a strange boy arrived.

"This is Ike." Mino giggled, covering her mouth with her hand. The move was adorable, her signature, and kryptonite to young men all around. Ike was clearly no exception.

"We only have two tickets," I whispered, sensing what was coming next.

"It's okay," she assured me. "He's just catching a ride uptown."

When we arrived at Radio City, Ike walked with us to the door, which made it very clear: he was not just riding uptown with us. He was taking my place.

"I'll put you in a cab home if we can't all get in," she said, affirming my fear. My little girl's desire for us to be together had nothing on her teenage dream of independence. But I would not give up.

My creativity kicking into high gear, I stacked the tickets to obscure the quantity, then handed them to the usher, smiling. "Here you go!"

He ripped the stubs off the two tickets and waved all three of us in. My trick had worked. Mino bought me Twizzlers. Ike high-fived me like I was the man, and I believed it, so long as I didn't think too hard about how, moments earlier, I had been nothing but a desperate child.

A few weeks later, Mino took her sneaking out to the next level and ran away. Unlike most teenagers on the run, however, she fled with a movie star via his private jet. Fortunately, the movie star returned her shortly after a stern call with my father and just in time for her Sweet Sixteen. The celebrity-packed affair occurred in a nightclub that she confusingly both frequented and was punished for frequenting. The movie star, who was banned from the event, sent sixteen dozen red roses in his stead. My dad banged out "You're Sixteen (You're Beautiful and You're Mine)" on the piano. The party carried on into the wee hours. I danced all night in Mary Janes and a ripped slip dress a few sizes too big. The straps kept falling, baring my flat chest to the rest of the party. But what did I care? I was bohemian! Fabulous! And at that time in New York City, nothing said that quite like dancing to hardcore rap in oversize antique underwear.

When Mino disappeared again a few years later, it wasn't as glamorous. Realizing she was gone, my mother woke me and my friend Bea in the middle of the night and piled us into a taxi. Bea was my best friend for a couple of reasons. Firstably, I couldn't really be friends with Tilly, since Tilly and

I were essentially fucking. And two, no matter how many rows between my parents she was subjected to, or how much I insisted we both sleep in my mother's bed to make her feel better afterward, Bea still said yes to playdates, a fact that mystifies me to this day.

That night we spent hours combing the city, in search of my missing sister and fearing the worst. When we finally found her, she was just a few blocks from our house, crying on a stoop next to a bodega. Empty bags of chips, a few boxes of Nilla wafers, and other delicious detritus surrounded her. We tried to goad her into the taxi, but she just kept shoving cookies in her mouth until the whole bag was finished. I found this disturbing. Why wasn't she saving any for me? I *loved* Nilla wafers and was never allowed them due to our mother's strict no-sugar rule.

"What is happening?" Bea whispered to me.

"Shut up," I said, as if I knew. With no younger sister of my own, Bea was the de facto heir to my superior attitude. In truth, I was jealous of her single-child status. Her life seemed so simple, even if her parents were divorced and my clothes were better.

Some weeks later, my family and I were driving through the Arizona desert in a rented yellow convertible, laughing and singing along to Steve Miller. It was almost as if we were on a normal family vacation, except our destination wasn't a water park or anything like that but a week of mandated family therapy at a rehab center, where Mino was undergoing treatment.

Apparently, my sister had BED, which incidentally wasn't just the place I enjoyed being snuggled by her, but also an acronym for Binge Eating Disorder. I thought this was weird. From what I knew of eating disorders, the whole point was you ate *less* so you got skinnier, not more, like Mino did, because that made you fat. Not to mention, by that time Mino was a model and model meant skinny. BED was an occupational hazard. Despite my confusion, I appreciated the opportunity for us all to be together, even if being eleven meant I couldn't attend grown-up therapy. But that was no matter: I got to be in my very *own* group with my very *own* counselor.

Even though Kim was an adult, she was smaller than I was because she had stunted her growth through an eating disorder, but the good kind that made you skinny. Fortunately, Kim was all better now. Her illness, however, had lasting effects: she was still so thin she couldn't sleep at night. Her spine poked into the mattress. Being skinny seemed really stressful. I wondered why everyone was so into it. Most especially my mom, who for a while set a large rubber replica of ten pounds' worth of fat in the middle of our dining room table for us all to behold as we ate dinner.

"I want you to be a lean, mean running machine," she said to me around that same time, while discussing my plans for that coming summer. All I'd wanted was to see the Spice Girls at Jones Beach. Which I did. Twice.

For the most part, I liked rehab. Kim let me drink as much lemonade as I wanted and eat saltines by the sleeve. We watched movies and petted horses and drew pictures. One day she asked me to draw a family. So I did. "The Monsters" were a fun bunch with absolutely no relation to my family, despite there being three daughters (the youngest, oddly, the only one who wasn't a monster and was obviously the prettiest), an older half brother, and two parents. They yelled a lot and had superpowers, which included an ability to cause horrific storms. They slept in gooey sacks. They loved each other.

When she told me to draw *my* family, I took a more figurative approach, rendering us as a solar system instead of people. We were all planets. Mino was the sun. But her star wasn't fixed. Anyone could be her. Anyone, it seemed, except me.

MY BLUE HEAVEN

One of the only reasons I did ballet was the vending machine in the dance studio's lobby. It had chocolate milk, the Hershey kind, which was my favorite. The other reason: Emi did ballet, and I wanted to be her, though I didn't want the eating disorder she was using ballet to cover. My time at Mino's rehab a few months earlier had made me wary of them, even the ones like Emi had that made you skinny. They seemed like a lot of work.

"A hundred, a hundred and one, a hundred and two," Emi would count breathlessly, as she attempted a thousand crunches daily. Her eyes glazed over with sad determination, while I watched confused, sucking on sugar cubes stolen from the pantry. Since Emi was a rotten bully, her suffering should have made me happy. Instead, the whole thing left me kind of embarrassed for her and unsure of my own trajectory. I didn't want to be like *that*. I would need a new calling. And thank God! I was tired of my teacher barking at me to tuck my "po-po" (Long Island for "potbelly," I believe). So tired, in fact, I started disappearing into the bathroom during classes, eventually leaving the building entirely. Braving the block and a half home, I'd sneak in through the basement to watch the Olsen twins on ABC. A much better way to spend the afternoon, if you ask me.

When my mother caught wind of my truancy, I was forced to take up a new after-school activity. After the traumatic loss of my hamster, Hamish, at the Jivamukti Center on Lafayette Street, there would be no more kids' yoga (though I did love the lying-down bit at the end). The only thing I liked about piano were the jelly beans, but the teacher only gave those out as a reward for practicing and I didn't, so that was that. Like a singer without a song, I was lost. Lost, until I discovered acting.

Emi's best friend was an actress and had already been in several films with stars like Tobey Maguire. In one movie, after he rejects her, she slaps her own face repeatedly, saying "I hate you" over and over in the mirror. Acting seemed like a good way to get attention for just being emotional instead of actually doing things. I knew I would be good at it. A few weeks later, I was enrolled in the SoHo Child Actor's Studio, which had no affiliation with the renowned Actors Studio but *was* in a studio apartment. The teacher, Dina, shared the place with her boyfriend, who I miraculously never saw, even though their bedroom was separated from the rest of the apartment only by a hole-filled paisley sheet. My mother entrusted me to Dina's care every Saturday from nine to one.

Mostly, we would do plays that were thinly veiled adaptations of famous movies. In my favorite, *Murder by Bequest*, a piece that was essentially a scene-for-scene copy of a popular Agatha Christie story, I played Methany Vixen. Methany was a hussy, which meant I got to wear a lot of Dina's clothes and makeup. Dina was very thin and wore high heels all the time. Her jeans were low-waisted, and she favored bedazzled low-cut tank tops. She was the perfect woman.

One day, as Dina was pressing a fake nail onto my thumb, she asked if I wanted to be a professional actress.

"Of course," I answered, almost before she could finish her question. "But I'd have to ask my mother."

"Okay. Ask her. I could be your manager."

By the time she'd finished her sentence, I'd all but quit the sixth grade and hired a personal assistant.

After that, at the end of our weekly classes, when all the other kids were slipping back into their shoes, I'd lounge conspicuously on Dina's futon, waiting for the poor suckers to ask me what I was doing.

"Oh, nothing," I'd lilt once they did. "Just working on my contemporary monologue."

Dina said I needed to have one of these "under my belt" to get an agent, which I would need to get a job, which I would need to get an MTV Movie Award. The monologue she selected was from a Tennessee Williams one-act that I was too young to actually read. From the little speech she cobbled together, however, it was clear: I was a child prostitute.

"Hi! I'm Willie," I yelled in a Southern accent as I steadied myself on imaginary train tracks. In my hands, I clutched a mildewed cloth doll. "Crazy Doll's hair needs washing," I said, before explaining how I ate food out of a garbage pail and went on dates with a "sup'rintendent!" 'cause my sister Alva was dead from some kind of infection and I'd taken on all her beaux. Then I'd say something about the movie *Camille*, get really sad, and sing *You're the only star in my blue heaven* to a vague melody, while staring into my doll's remaining eye. Finally, I would scream, "Not even a goddamn Victrola!" and begin to cry.

I performed the speech for whoever would listen. My mother loved it. My friend Mona, a sensible girl whose aunt was a real Hollywood actress, said I should have an Oscar. I disagreed. An Olivier, maybe. Or a Tony. But not an Oscar—not *yet*. I practiced and practiced, until the day came to do it for the professional agent.

Esther was the first adult I'd ever met who worked with children but didn't smile. She was also the only adult I'd ever met who had just one hand. She waved me into her office with it, then commanded me to begin my monologue. By the time I finished, I not only learned the sound of one hand clapping, I had also secured my very first agent.

"Welcome," she said in the same tone most would say "go away."

That week I had my photo taken by a professional photographer. I was told to wear black and hang off random city scaffoldings appearing hurt, stoic, and employable. We xeroxed the winning picture and I stapled my résumé to the back of eighty or so of them. Dina told me to fill it out with made-up jobs. I named my fake characters things like "Jancy" and "Water Gun Girl" and listed my special talents as riding horses, playing saxophone, and speaking Latin. I lied about my height and weight. I was a real actress.

At first my professional career went nowhere. Still, I continued to hone my skills in plays at school and camp, where, despite being a preteen, I found myself cast as even more ladies of the night. There was the Thai streetwalker in the ensemble of *Chess*. Clytemnestra, Agamemnon's sex slave, in my middle school's Greek festival. A slew of other promiscuous women: Mozart's loose wife in *Amadeus*. The silent, philandering one in Strindberg's *The Stronger*. More mature roles followed: a pregnant teenager in a play about the Troubles of Ireland. The father in *The Secret Garden*.

By the end of middle school, my experience paid off, and I secured my very first screen test. The movie was about a young brother and sister who rob a bank to save their family from financial ruin, and the studio flew me and my parents out to Los Angeles, where it was to take place. As I unpacked my Hello Kitty suitcase, it quickly became apparent that I had nothing to wear that would pass for "regular kid."

By that point, Emi had been dressing me for years. I wore snake-print miniskirts. Yellow and green fishnet stockings. Floral Dr. Martens. Hand-me-down tartan creepers. Vintage punk-band T-shirts (the Clash, the Circle Jerks, Crime). A suede cowgirl outfit. My hair in Princess Leia buns. The less it matched, the more Emi liked it. The more Emi liked it, the more I did.

Apparently, the newly minted *Teen Vogue* did too, so much so that they sent a photographer over to capture me in my natural habitat: the hot-pink and Stila body product–plastered bathroom Emi and I shared. Holding my cat, Hendrix, who hated me, I stood against my sink in a dress styled over jeans. Confident my uniqueness would cement me as a preteen idol, I was disappointed the following month when I discovered the "Letters to the Editor" section had published a few dissenting opinions.

"Why is she in her bathroom? Gross!" read one.

"Why is she wearing a kid's dress *and* jeans AT THE SAME TIME?!" wrote another.

In Los Angeles, hoping to avoid being further marooned by my family's eccentricities, I implored my mom to take me shopping somewhere normal like Limited Too. We went to Fred Segal. There, I got a pair of fancy two-hundred-dollar jeans that were too tight to sit down in and a bedazzled Led Zeppelin T-shirt with slits in the back. Needless to say, I didn't get the part. A young girl named Kristen Stewart did instead. I cried a river as I kissed my kid movie career goodbye.

A few nights later, a famous redheaded movie star was seated across from me at one of our family's dinner parties.

"You don't want that," she said.

I put my fork down quickly, believing she was referring to the potato at its end.

"You have to grow up first," she continued.

Ah, it was child stardom she was referring to. Gratefully, I shoved the potato in my mouth. But I couldn't help thinking she was a bit of a moron. Didn't she know how grown-up I was already?

THE SIMPLE LIFE

There were the little things—the turquoise bracelet my dad got me on tour out west, the one I wore so much a stone fell out. The miniature woven dolls you put under your pillow at night, who were supposed to abscond with your worries by the morning. Then there were the bigger things, like the framed autograph from Bon Jovi, my favorite singer, from the summer Tico Torres broke his arm and my dad filled in for him. For a long time, my father's absence just meant presents like these and getting to stay up late on the nights he came home. But in seventh grade, after I discovered a thread of secret emails he'd left open on my computer, I learned my father's absences meant a bit more: on the road, he led a double life. Sometimes even a triple.

While this was news to me, apparently, everyone else in the family had been in the know for a while. Now that I was in the loop, my mother had little issue seeking my advice.

"You either have to accept him as he is or just leave," I often found myself saying, though I still wasn't even sure how to correctly use a maxi pad.

"Right," she'd reply perfunctorily, her mind twisting around more exciting solutions, like a boob lift or burning all the nice sweaters she'd bought him.

"But if you burn the sweaters," I warned her, hoping I could reason her into being more reasonable, like Bea's mom, Carol, who made us breaded chicken and wore L.L.Bean, "he'll *definitely* cheat again."

Solving the problems of my parents' marriage was trying work, but it had to be done. While my father's actions were excruciating, witnessing the suffering they caused my mother was all the more so. Her pain flowed to me as easily as her bursts of joy flooded me. The cord between us was still intact. Whatever she felt, I did too. The connection was almost supernatural, like a phantom limb or long-lost twin. Impossibly, I'd attempt to placate her and soothe myself. Sleeping in her bed. Following her improvised rules. But it was no use. After all, I was not the source of her displeasure. He was. Her moods remained as mercurial as the summer sky in the South.

My father, for better or worse, was more consistent. He did yoga every morning and he loved *The Simpsons*. Whenever he was home, he made me two soft-boiled eggs with soldiers for breakfast and drove me to school. It was on one of these early morning commutes that I took the opportunity to get to the heart of the matter. "I just don't get it," I said between songs I'd ripped off LimeWire. He always let me DJ. "You said you wouldn't, remember?"

"Promises made in storms," he remarked, as he often did, "are always forgotten in calm waters."

I was dumbstruck at his ability to sound so profound and so lazy and all at once.

Fortunately, summer was soon upon us. While I could barely make it through a sleepover without calling someone to come pick me up at three a.m., I decided sleepaway camp would be a good idea. It seemed so American, something I was growing desperate to be, even if my family threw the word around like an insult. Americans, you see, were pure and wholesome. They wore one-pieces and smelled like sunscreen all summer. In stark contrast, my British family and I, who spent our Augusts topless on private beaches, doused in tanning oil (no SPF), were heathens. Fitting in with people who stood out so much was exhausting. Sleeping in neat rows of beds occupied by girls in matching bracelets and smelling of the same shampoo appealed to me. Sleepaway camp it was.

But which? Rose sent away for the VHS tapes camps used to use to advertise themselves. When they arrived, I ripped into their thick manila envelopes, impatient to discover the secrets of real American youth. At one camp, girls in shorts rolled over at the waist walked tightropes between trees. They spoke to the camera through colorful rubber-banded teeth about connections they'd never forget. Hard pass. At another, kids canoed until the early evening, then roasted marshmallows on open fires. Again, no. At yet another, they danced and sang. No, no, no. While I longed to love the great outdoors like other kids, frankly, my ideal summer consisted of sitting as close to the AC as possible, avoiding my mother's meltdowns, while watching reruns of *Ally McBeal*. But when I found a mysterious leaflet nestled beneath the mass of tapes, my interests were piqued.

Shamoo Farm was located near my favorite chocolate-themed amusement park in Pennsylvania. The girls who attended would be assigned care of a single animal and guaranteed entry into the regional farm show. In the habit of remedying my feeling of being an outsider by disguising myself as an insider, in Shamoo Farm, I smelled opportunity. There, I could finally resolve my English alienation by becoming like the all-American Fern, the heroine of *Charlotte's Web,* a book I had skimmed for school. A vision of myself as a knowledgeable farm girl began to unfurl. I would carry buckets up hills in mud-stained wellies. I would teach my animal to walk on its hind legs by gently hitting its front legs up with a cane. We would be best friends. I would win the farm show and be awarded a million dollars and a medal. My big-city woes would be resolved by simple country life. United by my success, my family would change for the better.

The deposit was sent in, and soon I'd be on my way. But not before a trip to a Park Avenue hypnotist, of course, to deal with my inevitable homesickness.

"Describe your favorite room," said the tweed-jacketed man from an Eames chair.

I described my therapist's office. Her Calder mobile. Her seasonal assortment of windowsill flora that resembled various genitalia. An hour later, I woke up. The hypnotist handed me a cassette and instructed me to listen to it before bed each night, to hypnotize myself out of being homesick. Clutching it like it was a key to freedom, I stepped out onto the tulip-lined street below. Normally, I hated the Upper East Side, finding it sterile, lifeless, and overpopulated by doctors. But that afternoon, through the lens of my new-found hope, I saw only its beauty.

Shortly after, my transformation from jaded city kid was underway . . . and dead on arrival. The whole camp reeked of shit. Our bunks had no real doors or windows, just screens. *And* the walls were painted purple, a color my mother loathed, which meant I did too. The depth of my homesickness as a child can only be likened to the romantic heartbreak I have felt as an adult: all harm was erased by distance. My heart only grew fonder. To add insult to injury, my friend Bea, who'd decided to come along, was "having a blast," which she told me about six times a day. There is nothing like another's enthusiasm for something you hate to really drive home the feeling of isolation. Not even the hypnotist's tape could rescue me. I spent most nights crying, falling asleep moments before they woke us at dawn.

When a batch of baby animals was born a week in, my hope was briefly restored. After all, winning a prize with a baby animal was why I'd chosen the camp in the first place. But when I saw the creatures, I felt only disgust. They were bony and coated in blood and guts. Plus: they were *calves*, and I wanted a pig, like Wilbur. Sensing my disinterest, Sharon, the camp's ruddy-faced head honcho, tried to engage me by letting me name one. The lone rule: it had to begin with a P for some stupid reason. P. P. P . . . My mom had a friend named Pamela who was very nice and pretty? I missed my mom so damn much. The calf would be named Pretty Pamela. For my mom's friend. Because I loved my mother and I never wanted to leave her side again. Abandoning my fantasy of rearing pigs like Fern, I set my sights on cattle. Pamela would be my vindication, my prizewinner. I'd have her walking on her hind legs in no time, and then me and my millions would get off this farm for good and ride into the sunset.

The work bell rang and reality set in yet again: it was back to shoveling shit. Knee-deep in a large room of manure, I shoveled poop from one corner to another, which seemed to accomplish absolutely nothing. I felt like Sisyphus, even though I had no idea who that was yet. At lunch, I tried to call home, only to be told campers weren't allowed to use the phone for another week. My depression deepened.

After supper, we sat in a circle to do Warm and Fuzzies. Warm and Fuzzies were anonymous notes campers tucked into a jar labeled "Warm and Fuzzy." They were supposed to be nice things you felt about fellow campers. Alternatively, they could be critiques you were afraid to voice aloud.

Jenna has nice hair.
Sam is fast at running.
Lola walks around naked.

It was true. Daily, I made the long walk to the shower from our bunk through the meadow barefoot in nothing but my towel, clutching my shampoo and conditioner to my chest. On good days, this left me feeling lithe, lyrical, and European. On others, it was clear: I didn't understand the unspoken rules of society. And I didn't have the right camp accoutrements. I didn't have Teen Spirit deodorant or little bras for nonexistent breasts. I had nothing anyone else had and one thing no one else did: a tape from a Park Avenue hypnotist. But I didn't care anymore about conforming to American life. I wanted out.

As soon as phone privileges were granted, I called home collect.

"Can you p-p-please come p-p-pick me up?" I stammered through tears as soon as my mother answered. Happy girls were playing leapfrog through a large window.

"Lola! No!"

I didn't care that she was telling me what I didn't want to hear. Her voice was so goddamn beautiful.

"Why?"

"It's too expensive. You said you wouldn't do this again."

She was right. I had sworn after a weeklong stint at another camp the summer prior. But promises made in calm waters . . .

My despondency had some upsides: Sharon took me off shit-shoveling duty and said I could spend more time with Pretty Pamela. I fantasized about outfits the calf could wear at the farm show. Perhaps a bowler hat. A monocle. But Pretty Pamela was useless, not even walking upright yet, and it had already been a week. Fortunately, there were other perks. Usually my mother didn't allow sugar of any kind, but my suffering had softened her hard line and she sent me a care package. In it, were Warheads. Airheads. Even a base-ball-size jawbreaker I'd been desperate to try from a local candy shop. Above all, there was a letter. In her handwriting. Her almost illegible handwriting. While it embarrassed me on notes to school because it looked like she wrote with her feet in the back of a moving car, from my distant perch in Pennsylvania, it brought only joy.

Don't eat them all at once!!! I love you. Mummy.

I clutched the note like a soldier in a foxhole might his girl's nudie picture.

One morning a few days later, we were woken earlier than usual.

"Lola's dad is here to pick her up!" said a counselor, likely more relieved than I was.

I was so happy to leave, I promised Sharon I'd be back the next summer. Bea, on the other hand, extended another two weeks; she was, after all, having a blast. As I watched the idyllic little farm grow smaller through the back window of my family's car, my spirits lifted. Still, I couldn't help but feel a little guilty for missing the farm show. I told myself Pretty Pamela would be fine without me. Better off, even. She deserved to be loved as she was. Not by someone like me, who was going to try to make her into something she wasn't.

I couldn't wait to get home. I didn't even care anymore that it wasn't the home I wished it was. As our car passed an Amish family in a buggy on the road beside us, I smiled at the grim-faced, bonneted little girl within. She did not smile back. Perhaps she sensed my condescension. My relief at not being her. Our vehicle quickly outpaced theirs. My dad let me pick the next song.

OBLIVION

Secretly, I liked Wanda, even though I wasn't supposed to. She seemed reasonable, at least more reasonable than my mother, who often made me call Wanda to demand that she stop her romantic relationship with my father.

"Tell her she's ruining your family!" my mother whispered one afternoon, a sad excitement in her eyes as she fed me lines from across the breakfast nook.

"She's ruining your family," I repeated into the receiver.

"NO! Tell *her* she's ruining *your* family!" my mother corrected.

"I'm sorry, Wanda, I meant *you're* ruining *my* family."

Wanda sighed into the receiver, miserable as any mistress might be talking to their lover's adolescent daughter. A warped antique painting of a naked woman watched over me. She was skinny and alone—just how I pictured Wanda.

"Anyhoo, it must be late there," I continued, aware she was somewhere across the pond. "I'll let you go now."

"You know, Lola," Wanda chimed in as I was about to hang up, "you seem like a lovely girl."

"Thank you," I replied. A sucker for approval, I couldn't help but smile, which alarmed my mother.

"What's happening?" she whisper-yelled across the table.

"I think we would get on wonderfully. I could be a great mum to you," Wanda continued.

I was grateful when my mother disconnected the call.

"What on earth was she saying?" my mom demanded.

"That she was really sorry," I lied. I knew the truth would only hurt her.

The revelation of my father's infidelity a year earlier had confirmed the thing I'd feared most for the majority of my life: that our ferocious kind of love was just plain ferocity. That my family was an unhappy one.

In search of true love and happiness, I began to pull away and to spend more time with friends, like Bettina Richards-Goldblatt.

Bettina lived on the other side of the fence from us in East Hampton. While we were nemeses during the school year in the city, we were unlikely friends as neighbors over summers on Long Island, due to our clear quid pro quo arrangement: she could jump on *my* trampoline (her father was a surgeon who had seen a few too many broken limbs), while I could eat all of *her* junk food (my mother had seen a few too many thinner women flirt with her husband and refused to keep sugar in the house). Under the guise of amiability, we cut a hole in the chicken-wire fence that divided our properties to allow for swift passage.

Initially a terrifying tomboy, over time Bettina had grown increasingly less interested in sports and more interested in her looks. She was extremely confident and would always talk about how beautiful she was. She even started paying me compliments, one time telling me I had "DSL" (dick-sucking lips) before promptly reminding me that she had nicer eyes and hair. Her nanny, Shayla, preempted Bettina's physical development by purchasing her a bra that generously gathered her chest fat into breast-like mounds. She was becoming so grown up, just like I wanted to be and secretly felt I already was. After all, I'd spent much of middle school acting as my parents' marriage counselor and at least one spring break at rehab. If other kids did that too, I certainly didn't know them.

One day I noticed Bettina's ears wiggling while we were watching TV.

"You can wiggle your ears?" I asked, amazed.

"Oh," she said, giggling girlishly, "I'm actually doing my Kegels."

My mother wasn't quite as sold on Bettina as I was. To sway her, I'd tell her things I thought she'd find impressive, like how much Bettina's house cost.

"Twelve million dollars."

"Really?" She looked disturbed.

"And another twelve million for the property!" I bragged.

"Well, it's ugly," she said.

"How much did our house cost?"

While we were wealthy, we weren't Bettina wealthy. My mom didn't answer.

One summer afternoon, I emerged from digging around Bettina's oversized fridge to discover her swimming pool, usually crawling with kids, completely empty. Armed with a bag of Oreo Minis I'd pilfered from her pantry, I wandered upstairs to discover a trail of girls from Bettina's day camp lined up outside her bathroom door.

"You *guys*," I announced myself, "what are you doing?"

"Shhhh!" they all hissed through retainers I envied.

Suddenly, Bettina flung the door open. "Ugh! I'm so re-freshed!"

"'Cause you showered?" I asked, confused.

"No, idiot." She grabbed my wrist and yanked me into the bathroom, then lay down in the tub. Spreading her legs wide on either side of the faucet, she turned it on, letting the water spill into her crotch. "But you don't want it too hot!" she admonished.

Within seconds, her hips were pulsing in a strange rhythm, and she was laughing maniacally. This disturbed me.

"What? Samantha from *Sex and the City* does it," she

said, disgusted by my disgust. She turned the taps off. I ran home through the hole in the fence.

After dinner with some family friends that evening, I asked Harry, a boy one year my senior, to take a walk with me to the basketball court. With a pubescent tuft of hair on his neck like a billy goat's and a rotation of board shorts with different rock stars printed on them, he was, to me, the epitome of sage. He shot hoops as I told him what I had seen.

"Dude." His voice cracked. "Masturbation is THE BEST. You gotta try it."

The faucet on my antique bathtub resembled a sawed-off shotgun. Its water always smelled like rust, and its pressure had only two crude modes: off and full on. It was nothing like Bettina's. Still, I would make do, locking the door and closing the curtain before lowering myself into its depths. Once I did, I couldn't help but feel much the way I do now whenever I'm about to have sex: large. With my legs spread and lying back, I saw highlighted the things I was growing to dislike most about my body. The rolls in my stomach. My increasing thighs. I envisioned the double chin my faucet saw. A few seconds after I'd turned the water on, things changed. My body cramped and seized until it entered a fugue state. Minutes later, I was at it again.

I spent the rest of the summer either doing exactly this

or figuring out ways I could. My interest in Bettina's snacks was quickly replaced by an intense romance with the jets in her pool. Pretty much any time I was alone or shrouded in darkness, my hand was in my pants. Even during films like *What a Girl Wants* and *The Life of David Gale*. I was sick. An addict.

Apparently, my father was too, which explained things a little.

"Where is he?" I asked my mother one afternoon that fall. It had been days since I'd seen him.

"Rehab," she said, lighting a cigarette as she kicked her feet up on her desk.

"Did he start drinking again?" I asked, surprised. He'd been sober for so long.

After a few quick pulls, she stubbed out her Marlboro Light so forcefully it broke in half, then rolled her eyes as if to say, *Once an addict, always an addict.* In that moment it was clear: I had a long, arduous road ahead of me.

That Christmas, we traveled to a spa in southern India. Upon arrival, we had to fill out forms about our health. As I made my way through the questionnaire, I was stunned to discover a question asking me to rank my sex drive. Torn about whether to lie, I ultimately decided that, were I to receive the support I needed, honesty was the best policy: sure, I was a twelve-year-old virgin, but my sex drive was an 11 out of 10. Perhaps they could help.

When I realized the doctors were going to read the questionnaires back to us in front of the whole family, I regretted my transparency.

"May I just fix one thing?" I asked, trying to snatch the clipboard back from the Ayurvedic doctor. Fortunately, my father intervened.

"Enough already," he said protectively. My eyes caught his. As soon as they did, I looked away. I was grateful that my father understood me. I was also mortified.

The week continued with yoga at dawn and dinners of orange peels. It was all tremendously unfun, though I had come to accept the trip as penance for my sins. When New Year's Eve rolled around, however, I wanted to party—or at least my version of party back then, which is strikingly similar to my version of party now minus four martinis: get dressed up, talk, and eat candy. But Emi had disappeared with a group of local teenage boys to go smoke hashish, and everyone else had gone to sleep at sunset. I had no one to talk to, and there certainly wasn't any candy.

Sensing my restlessness, my father agreed to stay up with me while I sounded a noisemaker I'd found at the front desk and ran around the wide hotel hallways in my party dress. Finally, the clock struck midnight.

"All right, darling," he said, yawning with relief.

"Just a second," I replied, steadying myself before a large window. Overlooking the dark ocean, I tried to feel the excitement of it all. A new year was beginning. I would be another year older, another year closer to the grown-up I was so desperate to become. But in that moment, all I wanted was for time to stop, so I could be a kid again, or as I never really was, and forever.

MARLBORO GIRL

My first relationship was just four hours long. In hindsight, it was stupid of me to end it: not only was he *gorgeous*, he was also the heir to a vast tabloid fortune. It all began on an early summer's afternoon, at the base of one of his Amagansett estate's many fountains.

"Do you wanna go out?" my suave preteen paramour asked, craning his neck to look up at me. Though we were both twelve, I'd hit puberty first and had about a foot on him.

I giggled, covering my mouth with my hand, the attractive way I'd observed Mino do around men, hoping to project some of her charm and ensure he wouldn't see I was eating some cheese.

"Yes!" I replied. A little piece flew out.

Officially BF and GF, he grabbed my free hand and held it tight, whisking me all the way up his home's interminable driveway from the pool house to the main house in time for his staff to serve us lunch. Having removed my shoes to make our height discrepancy less obvious, I tried to act like the gravel wasn't painful on my bare feet. Fortunately, he didn't seem to notice. He was just smitten. Naturally. When we finally arrived, I tried to pull my hand away before his mother saw us. But he just held it tight. He saw no reason our love should be discreet. We were together now, "a thing." And there was nothing wrong with that. Except that I found it mildly disgusting.

I had spent most of my childhood wishing I were grown up, so I might be included in all the grown-up happenings around me. But also so when my parents inevitably *did* include me in decidedly adult things, it wouldn't feel so wrong. Now that I was finally maturing, I wanted none of it. Since India, I'd been tortured by the notion that my youth was fleeting. I feared adulthood might mean even more distance between myself and the family I had always longed to be closer to.

My mother, it seemed, shared in my anxiety. While her actions often expedited my evolution, her words insisted otherwise.

"Aren't you a bit young for that?" she'd say if, for instance, a friend of mine was a grade or so older.

"That's too old for your age," she'd remark if I made a raunchy joke.

"That's not *age-appropriate!*"

Between me giving her marital advice and comments like these, I had no idea what age I was supposed to be. All I knew was she wouldn't approve of my newfound coupled status. Boyfriends were much too grown-up. Dead set on her approval, I decided to end it and fast.

"I don't think we should do this," I whispered later that night into the cordless phone I'd smuggled into my bathroom.

There was a long silence. "Is this because of your mom?" he said finally.

"No!" I lied.

A few weeks later, the tabloid heir licked his wounds and started dating Bea. While this made me briefly hate her, my ex and I remained close friends. One evening the two of us were hanging out in his hot tub when my older sister Emi slinked over with his older brother.

"Do you guys smoke?" Emi asked, standing straight up in the dark bubbling water, looking like a sexy teenage shark.

"No. We're *twelve*," I replied.

I hated smoking. It made everyone's breath bad and ruined the good-only-to-me smell of my baby blanket—a gorgeous Balinese sarong of Emi's I smothered myself with nightly. When my mom smoked in the car with all the windows up, I'd learned to protect the blanket from the stench by tucking it beneath my squeezed-shut thighs, spraying it tirelessly with my pink Fiorucci perfume once we were home.

"But the Strokes smoke," Emi said, as if I were the world's greatest hypocrite.

Urgently, I reached for the cigarette. I loved Julian Casablancas more than I loved my parents. Honestly, I don't know why it hadn't occurred to me to start smoking sooner. After one puff, it crumbled in my wet hands and fell to its untimely death in the water below.

"Idiot," Emi said.

In the moonlight, I could make out the shape of her bare breasts and perfect abs. I sank deeper into the hot tub, hoping to obscure my tummy. She swam away. The beautiful boys followed in her wake.

The next morning, my mother came in to wake me as she did most mornings: by yelling at me to clean my room before the cleaners came.

"And I heard you were smoking!" she tacked on to her usual "This room must be immaculate!"

"How?" I asked, as I coughed up a hunk of brown phlegm with a little blood in it.

"Your sister told me!"

That bitch. Since smoking seemed like it would cause even more trouble at home, I decided against it. I'd make Mona take it up instead.

Mona was my new best friend. At five-three, Mona was even taller than I was, which made her the tallest twelve-year-old I'd ever known. She was also the first person I'd heard describe herself as "anxious," and this was back *before* it was even a fad.

"Smoking helps that," I encouraged, clueless as a 1950s doctor conversing with a pregnant housewife. While I wanted her to feel better, the act wasn't without motive. I was eager to dilute her innate sensibility—a quality of hers that I both adore and deplore to this day, as it often only makes me seem even more insane.

Our work began in Emi's room, since even though Emi was still a teenager, she was allowed to smoke in there.

"Lay back on the chaise longue," I instructed Mona, who was holding a Camel Light we'd stolen days earlier in preparation. She did. I struck a match.

"It *is* weird," she said, exhaling a cloud of smoke with aplomb. "Like I actually *do* feel less anxious!"

"Right?" I remarked in enthusiastic agreement. My plan was working.

Together, we toiled at the habit until she became a natural. I'm not sure it eased her anxiety much, but it certainly added to her popularity at school, giving her inherent likability the edge she needed to become an indestructible force of the social scene. By the time we got to high school a couple years later, she had more friends than I did. Like *a lot* more. I reconsidered my ambivalence and bought a pack of Marlboro Reds.

By the tenth grade, I was a full-blown smoker. Sometimes I'd get grounded for it. Other times my mother didn't seem to mind. When I'd come home devastated by teenage heartache, she'd dangle a Marlboro Light before me, the way she once had my pacifier. Sometimes we smoked together. Other times she'd realize the error of her ways, confiscate mine, and smoke them herself.

By the time I hit eleventh grade, my mom decided I should quit.

"But *you* smoke!" I squawked.

"No, I don't!" she said, exhaling furiously before decimating her Marlboro in the ashtray.

That weekend, while most of my friends were enrolled in SAT prep, I was the only patron under forty attending a seven-hour seminar on smoking cessation.

"Cigarettes are just two-inch sticks of vegetable matter," said the small British man leading the course.

A picture of James Dean holding a cigarette lit up the screen behind him. The word "COOL" burned across it. The man clicked a button to go to the next slide, which was the same photo, just with the cigarette photoshopped out.

"STILL COOL," it read beneath. The whole room gasped at the magic.

"Without cigarettes," he promised us, "you'll still be cool. And—you'll be *free*."

I had always wondered about freedom. I knew my privilege was a kind of freedom. But most of the privileged people I knew didn't seem very free. They *all* smoked. Perhaps privilege wasn't a kind of freedom after all. Or maybe it was just a very privileged thing to squander your freedom. After all, you could always get more.

That afternoon, I resolved to leave the room a truly free woman. The wind in the sails of my sister's leather jacket pushed me down Lexington Avenue. I felt like I was flying.

I was smoking again a few days later.

NEVER LEARN NOT TO LOVE

My ninth-grade term-paper assignment was broad, but not broad enough to hide the fact that I hadn't paid attention in class. At all.

"Expound upon a pivotal event from the 20th Century," read a note I had written in bubble font with a silver-sparkle gel pen I was very into. So into, it seemed, that the rest of the page was an intricate doodle of a horse-man-cat wearing extremely cool sunglasses. I wracked my brain for something I could write about, something I could really sink my teeth into, but couldn't think of a single pivotal event from the twentieth century other than my birth. And *maybe* Charles Manson.

My long-haired hippie history teacher had spent a brief moment on the Manson Family to illustrate a larger point about something else I'd completely forgotten. But the pull of sex, death, and rock and roll was strong enough to ensure my memory of Manson stayed. I had my subject. Perhaps I wouldn't be kicked out of this school for underperformance, the way I almost was the last one after failing gym twice.

At dinner that evening, I told my family about the assignment and was surprised to find Emi excited. Since enthusiasm for me was a rare state for her, I suspected the subject was somehow personally relevant. It was.

"You *have* to interview Gustave!" she said, slurping her zucchini soup.

Gustave was a filmmaker. His most famous movie was a cult classic, starring him as a man who kidnaps a young dancer and forces her to drive all the way to Buffalo to meet his parents. Incidentally, Emi, taking time off from her freshman year at the Rhode Island School of Design (RISD), had just been on a similar trip with him, though she'd gone willingly.

"I'll give you his number. I'm sure he'd *love* to talk to you."

The following afternoon, I rang him up. "Hi," I said, trying to sound professional. "This is Emi's associate Lola. She mentioned you knew something about Manson?"

Gustave's only actual connection to the crimes was that he'd spent years collecting various memorabilia associated with them. He'd also written a script in which he would play Manson.

"So it starts like the most beautiful thing you've ever seen," he explained in a high, nasal voice. "Naked girls, daisies, the desert. Everyone's just having so much fun, and then—BAM! Blood! Sex! Violence!"

"Got it," I said, hanging on to every word, dutifully committing them to my stenographer's notebook in neon gel.

A few hours later, we were still on the phone, discussing the possibility of my starring in a music video he was directing and co-curating a music festival in England.

"Would you like that?" he asked.

"Absolutely!" I replied. "I'll go ask my mother."

When she said no, I was secretly relieved. Throwing a music festival sounded like a lot of work.

My history teacher was equally unimpressed.

"This isn't an interview about the event," he said, trying to make out my glittery lime green scrawl. "This is a transcription of a conversation about a movie that doesn't exist and band ideas for a music festival you're curating."

"But what if we got Simon and Garfunkel?" I said, attempting to sell him on it. He was a *huge* fan.

"They haven't played together for years," he replied sadly.

Despite all my best efforts, I was still at square one and in need of a more informed grown-up to talk to. Then I remembered: Poppy, Bea's grandfather. While the women in my family mostly treated my friend Bea like "OPK"—

other people's kids—Bea's family always treated me as if I were their own. I loved her grandfather so much, I sometimes wondered if there was something romantic between us. Then I learned he was gay. Regardless, he was my type: whatever the occasion, he was dependably dressed in a three-piece suit and doused in Chanel No. 5. He loved to sing Marilyn Monroe songs, and he winked a lot. My dream man.

"Poppy—" I beamed into the phone the next day.

"Yes, dear?"

"Could I please interview you about Charles Manson?"

"Oh, honey, of course you could, but you know . . . you really ought to talk to Bea's aunt Joan about all that."

Aunt Joan was the woman uptown Bea and I spent Easters with. She was frail with an immovable bob and I'd never heard her speak. She seemed mean. Crestfallen, I took down her number.

The next day, I rode the 4 to the 6 all the way from my school in Brooklyn to Aunt Joan's apartment in the mid-Sixties. Like her, it was prim and clean and quiet, with an air of sadness draped over it. She wore a floral dress like a little girl and served me tea and baklava she'd arranged on pretty china. Her skin looked like wet paper. In a tiny voice, she explained how she had lived with one of the Manson girls after the murders, in witness protection.

She even met Manson once before the murders, picking him up hitchhiking. I tried to picture this old woman with frightened blue eyes young, hip, and picking up hitchhikers. I couldn't.

My imagination wasn't the only thing that was stunted. I was an ungifted interviewer, mostly asking if she might repeat herself instead of anything substantial because her voice was so soft. I could barely even work the tape recorder. But Aunt Joan was encouraging, eventually leading me into a small pantry where, instead of food, she kept books. From a high shelf she reached via a terrifyingly precarious step stool, she pulled down a few pulpy first editions on Manson. Their covers looked as if they'd been dipped in acid. Text dripped. Swastikas and boobies glowed in hot pink.

"Keep these," she said, her voice trembling. I accepted them gratefully, even though I knew, no matter how cool they looked, I likely wouldn't read them. At that time, I had yet to wholly subscribe to the notion that I had to do extra things to make me fabulous. Believing already that I sort of just was, I was terribly lazy.

When we reemerged from the book pantry, the living room was gold from the setting sun, making it clear: it was time to leave. I imagined she must be exhausted anyway. Not only had she spent hours acting as if I weren't a tremendous waste of time, but she was also grieving: her husband and her daughter had both just died within a couple years of each other. Bea had told me not to mention it so I tried to convey my condolences with the tightest possible hug good-bye. In return, she patted me on the back, politely maintaining a foot of space between us as she did. I marveled at her strength.

In college a while later, I noticed the ultimate accoutrement to being a beautiful, cool, smart liberal arts girl was a well-loved copy of a particular book. Eager to achieve that same je ne sais quoi as my peers, I went in for deeper inspection when I saw Joan's name across the top. When I made the connection, I felt like a fool. I hadn't just interviewed Bea's old Aunt Joan. I had interviewed *Joan Didion*, one of the most important writers of our time, for one of the worst pieces of writing in history. "The Hippie Who Killed the Sixties" was an awful paper. My school didn't have grades, but if it had, I'm sure I wouldn't have even gotten a D and that only because she had been involved.

That fall break, I scrounged through my drawers in search of this precious tape. Underneath old dime bags and diaries I had started and then abandoned, I found it: "Lola interviews Bea's old aunt."

Sticking it in my tape recorder, I waited excitedly for it to rewind. When it was ready, I hit play and sat back to listen as Joan Didion spoke to me.

"You know, Lola," she began to say, "and this is something just simply remarkable—"

But before she could finish, Mino's voice cut her off. She was trilling. Tra-la-la-ing. Practicing vocal scales. Erasing Joan Didion's words with every note, like an ambulance outside the symphony.

DESIRE

Eve was an actress who lived uptown and scared the shit out of me. Still, despite her being Mona's aunt and my mother's friend, we had grown close over the previous summer. Lonely because her own children were with their father for the season, she'd often pick me up from my job as a hapless day-camp counselor. Then, as we inched down back roads in her classic GTO, a convertible she was too scared to actually drive, I'd talk her out of panic attacks caused by some asshole behind us in a G-wagon. In turn, she'd regale me with stories about famous men—who had a big dick, who was a bad lover, who was a general piece of shit, etc. Six hours and three miles later, we'd finally reach our destination: her Long Island estate, a sprawling home she slinked about like an exotic cat, smelling of thick musk and wearing loose Pucci.

Eve had acted since she was young, making her way out of the Bronx by waitressing at Max's Kansas City before hitting it big in Hollywood. Eventually, she married a man who looked like Humpty-Dumpty and made his fortune selling antiperspirant and vehicles used for the war in Afghanistan. For him, she had given up acting. In return, she received a score of closets that were bigger than most New York apartments. Since these were the only spaces in the houses that were truly hers, that was where we spent our time together, mostly working on auditions for my school plays. One afternoon, in her Manhattan closet, I was trying my hand at Olivia's monologue from *Twelfth Night*.

"Stop," she said bluntly, halfway through what I believed to be an Oscar-worthy performance. At the very least, a Golden Globe. "What's your intention?"

"To get the lead?"

No freshman had ever been awarded the lead in a high school play. I hoped to be the exception.

"No, dumbass," she said. "*In the play*."

We spent the next hour lightening my arm hair with an expensive French bleach, dividing the monologue into different sections and writing down verbs next to them. *To cajole. To seduce. To mollify.*

The reason we did this was that apparently characters, like people, had objectives, which were connected to their desires, and used various tactics—in the form of verbs—to achieve them. This made sense to me: *my* objective (to get the lead) was connected to my *desire* (to make everyone feel stupid for ever doubting me). But what tactics was I employing? *To charm? To obey? To be darling?* Were any of them actually working? Evidently not: after all our hard work, I rated only a made-up role I had to share with Mona. Since my high school's version of *Twelfth Night* was set in a funky circus world, the part happened to be that of a two-headed woman. Hardly what I'd had in mind, to say the least.

Eve and I continued our studies no matter the obstacle, not even breaking when I was hospitalized for Lyme disease later that year. At Mount Sinai, we tore through classic films she'd brought for us to watch on the small hospital TV. There was *Whatever Happened to Baby Jane?*, which I liked because it reminded me of myself and Emi. *Splendor in the Grass*, which made me weep for days. I could understand Warren Beatty's sexual frustration, Natalie Wood's abject hysteria. I could understand it because I felt that way about Eve's son, Jude.

At sixteen, Jude was an older man, a year my senior. He wore a different vintage band T-shirt every day, skinny jeans, and a dirty leather bracelet I sometimes saw him quietly pet for comfort. Jude was like the Skipper to Julian Casablancas's Barbie—my kryptonite. When Eve and Humpty inevitably split, she moved herself and Jude into our West Village home. No day had ever been greater.

Sometimes Jude loved me back. Other times not so much. With our rooms right next to each other, I had unmitigated access to staring at him while he practiced scales on an unamplified electric guitar.

"You sound *so good,*" I'd say from the doorway, even though I wasn't sure he did. Eventually, my flattery worked, and I became Jude's girlfriend, a position I gathered was quite competitive. Once, at a New Year's party on his ex-stepdad's yacht, a young starlet who was a decade older lured Jude toward her, and away from me, with a simple wave of her index finger.

"Here's your New Year's kiss, baby," I watched her say as she pulled his mouth to hers.

Didn't she know I had already given him one? Jude was mine. Or so I thought, until Blanche informed me otherwise.

Growing up, Blanche, who was a bit older, had been friends with both of my sisters. Even though she had been raised just down the street, she sounded like she was either from Brooklyn or Belgium or both. Long legged and short torsoed, Blanche wore scarves as dresses, underwear as shorts, and smoked cigarettes for breakfast, lunch, and dinner. I both adored and feared her: her main mode of expressing affection was by painfully pinching my face and stomach, then taking me for drinks at the restaurant around the corner.

One night, after coming to see me in my school's neo-futurist production of *Macbeth*, Blanche took me for Manhattans. As she detailed the highlights of my performance, I felt moved by how much interest she'd taken in my acting—especially since neither of my sisters ever really had.

Well, except for Emi one time, and that had gone very badly. Back from her freshman year at RISD and armed with a six-pack, Emi got my eighth-grade boyfriend and best guy friend so drunk before my star turn as the father in *The Secret Garden* that the two boys got caught fooling around in a bathroom stall a few hours later. Subsequently, they were both expelled.

That night at the bar, the conversation evolved as we finished our drinks.

"What's Jude's penis like?" Blanche asked suddenly, apropos of nothing.

Though I was aware that cool older women in my world casually rattled off details like dick size, it felt awkward to me.

"I've never seen it!" I lied.

She continued to ask me this same question for months, until I told her that it was perfectly nice. Her eyes lit up. I knew I had made a mistake.

One dark winter evening later that year, as I ascended my stoop, Blanche popped out from the shadows of our home's basement entrance.

"Can I come in?" she asked, which surprised me. Our friendship had seemingly gone cold after she complained I talked too much during a documentary about a man who gets eaten by grizzly bears. It had been a while since I'd seen her. Nevertheless, I obliged.

The place was empty except for us. Eve and Jude had moved to a twin brownstone nearby, and everyone in my family was either at Barneys, RISD, or rehab.

Blanche plopped down at the head of the dining table, then lit the cigarette she was having for dinner.

"So, you did not tell me that Jude's penis is *huge!*" she said with her strange guttural laugh. Stunned as I was, I was determined to play the cool woman of the world I believed I had to be around her.

"Who told you that?" I replied, feigning nonchalance.

"Emi," Blanche said. "You know she blew him, right? In your pool house? Last summer?"

A cloud of smoke hung in the air between us, making a figure eight before it vanished. I said nothing.

"But don't tell her I told you!" Blanche admonished, stubbing her cigarette out in a scented candle before disappearing back out into the darkness from which she came.

At first, I didn't believe her. Her objective, I was certain, was only to hurt me, to fulfill her desire of making me as miserable as she was. No wonder she wanted to hang out with me. My sisters would not tolerate her. No one her own age would. She had to prey on children. But a moment later, it occurred to me that she might have intended otherwise: perhaps Blanche was trying to help me the hard way, exposing me to yet another painful truth about my family.

For years, I'd watched my sisters swap boyfriends. Still, I'd never fathomed that the day would come when they set their sights on one of mine. This wasn't because I fancied myself special or anything, but because our age differences (almost six and eight years, respectively) made it seem technically impossible. Love was the one area of my life where I'd assumed my youth would protect instead of destroy me. But maybe I had been wrong: maybe in our family, age truly counted for nothing. Love had no bounds.

In a state of rage so advanced I felt calm, I floated toward the kitchen phone and dialed Emi, who by that time was back in Providence.

"Hello?" she answered. As soon as she did, my mind drew a blank. What words were appropriate for a situation that felt so very inappropriate? I remained silent.

"Is this *Randy*?" she said. I said nothing still. Until it came to me.

"Cunt."

The word fell quietly out of my mouth. While I had never actually used it before, I knew it meant serious business after my mom had slapped Mino for saying it to Emi at a ski resort years earlier.

So I kept serving it, in a fugue state.

Cunt. CUNT. YOU FUCKING CUNT.
CUNTTTTTTT!

Emi laughed then hung up on me. Alone again, I felt cold with failure, able only to warm myself with this thought: *When I become a successful actress, Emi will feel so stupid that she ever did anything as horrid as blow my teenage boyfriend in our family pool house and she'll be very, very sorry.*

A few years later, Emi, who hadn't ever wanted to be an actress, became the breakout star of a hit TV show, and long before I'd have any real acting jobs of my own. Fortunately by that time I knew: I didn't need to be more successful than my sister to know she was sorry. It just would have been a nice perk.

ROSE TATTOO

Rose's wedding day was one of the best and worst days of my life. The best because it meant she might finally find the happiness she deserved and have a family of her own. The worst for the exact same reason.

Rose was not my best friend, nor was she even technically related to me. Rose was better: she was my nanny. Dependable. Mutable. Mine. Rose was so adept at caring for me, it took growing up for me to realize she was paid to do it. Not only did we share interests, like shit-stirring in early AOL chat rooms, listening to the Spice Girls, and watching reruns of *Law & Order: Special Victims Unit*, we also shared bedrooms and the back-back row of my family's Mercedes station wagon, the foldout seats that faced the wrong way and made you sick when you went long distances. Where I went, Rose went. A constant in my turbulent world, Rose was like home. Welsh and round and blond, with a rose tattoo on her bum, Rose was different from the thin, exotic-looking women in my brood. Since I felt different too, I often felt like we were the same.

As I matured, things began to shift. It felt silly having her with me on the subway when I could ride alone. At my side, indulging in the occasional episode of *COPS* when no one was home. Our sameness was changing. By the time I was in eighth grade, our time together was whittled down to just summers. When that September rolled around and it was time for her to schlep her suitcases across trains, planes, and continents all the way back to Wales, I was inconsolable. Not because I needed her, as I once had, but because I didn't anymore. I was overcome with grief but also guilt: what if she still needed me? She didn't have children of her own to take care of her, the way I often felt I took care of my mother. I did some quick math. Rose's biological clock was running out. I feared I'd taken the best years of her life already.

To my relief, when Rose returned the following summer, she announced she was engaged. While Phil was a decade younger, which I found impressive, he was a truck driver, which was not exactly what I had in mind, but fine. With a new husband, I believed, if she acted fast, she could make up for the time she'd sacrificed for me, and I'd be off the hook. With haste, my family and I went about the arrangements for the ceremony. For Rose's gown, my mom and I selected a chic black cocktail dress with white beaded trim in the shape of small flowers. G and I decorated the back of his truck with cans of her favorite beer tied to strings. Emi wrote "Just Married" in paint on the back window. We drove Rose to the East Hampton court-house and played "Chapel of Love" on a CD Mino burned, on repeat, the whole way.

When we arrived, I was a little underwhelmed by Phil's attire: a rumpled white button-down shirt tucked into some Dockers. But Rose seemed happy so I let it slide. We threw rice from plastic bags as they descended the courthouse steps. I wiped tears from my face with the back of my hand like in the movies. But it was still real life, and the truth was, as grateful as I felt for Rose's fortune, I knew it meant more change. Who would we be to each other when she wasn't paid to take care of me? The empty cans clinked, and they pulled away. My despair deepened.

Fortunately, Phil and Rose were just going back to our house because Rose was still on the clock. Their reception was short-lived: a couple of Coronas on the couch in front of the telly, which they drank quickly, knowing well my mother's intolerance for beer and sitting down—other people relaxing always making her anxious. Given the circum-stances, this bothered me. Rose should celebrate, I thought, and started up the stairs to tell my mother as much, when Rose stopped me.

"Your mum got me the best gift," she defended. Despite how often Rose betrayed my mom and her no-sugar policy by smuggling me Cadbury's from across the Atlantic, then instructing me to "hide the evidence"—i.e., throw the candy wrappers in the trash on the street like a murder weapon—she was always standing up for her.

"What?" I asked.

"A thousand dollars," Rose said, her eyes welling, "to *Kmart.*"

"*Kmart?!*" I scoffed before correcting myself. I knew she loved that place. "What are you gonna spend it on?"

"I'm going to save it." She smiled, her eyes misty with hope. "For a baby."

Rose came back to the States the following summer but not to look after me. She'd taken another nannying job for a Real Housewife with younger children. The summer after, she was back again, this time with a movie star and her young son. Sometimes I'd drop by the actress's West Village brownstone after school to say hi. But it felt strange watching Rose chase other kids around, put on the same funny voices.

Eventually, Rose went back to Wales altogether and I saw her only when she rode the bus in to see me on family visits to London.

"So, how's being home?" I inquired on one such trip. Part of me hoped she'd say she wasn't home, because *I* was her home, but she didn't. It was fine, she said instead. Good to be near to her mum and dad and her sisters. It occurred to me in that moment that I knew nothing about Rose's family. How strange, I thought, when she knew everything about mine. What were her parents' names? How many sisters exactly did she have? Instead of asking, I changed the subject.

How was Phil? He was fine, she said. Our conversation was growing awkward. Work? All right. What did she do now? She told me she was getting up every morning at three a.m., to work in a factory kitchen.

"You don't have to wear a *hairnet*, do you?" I asked.

"Course I do, you blummin' nincompoop!"

I felt scandalized. I wanted to rescue her. To restore her to the comforts of those West Village brownstones and Hamptons summer homes she'd spent so much time in. But was that really saving her? Or had she just been so adept at saving me? The gaps between Rose's life and my own felt wider than ever.

A few years later, my sisters and I found a small way to close them: getting Rose's tattoo inked onto us.

I showed Rose our little tribute on another family trip to London shortly after, while sharing a cab with her and my mother.

"Blummin' hell!" she gasped before breaking down into tears, the gesture overwhelming her.

"Oh, Rose!" I said, attempting to console her. "I didn't mean to make you cry!"

"I was there!" my mother yelled suddenly from across the taxi.

For a moment Rose and I said nothing.

"I was there!" my mother repeated.

"*Where?*" Rose asked, confused.

"I think she means like when I was growing up?" I said before turning to my mother. She looked distraught. "I know, Mama," I said.

My mother looked back down at her phone. I felt stupid that I hadn't considered how the tattoo might make her feel. But I didn't think I needed a tattoo to keep myself bound to my mom. She was embedded in my DNA. I was just beginning to consider how much it would hurt to get MOTHER inked in bold across my forehead, when Rose disrupted me.

"That's where they jump out of," she said with a knowing look, pointing toward a patch of grass beyond the highway.

"Who?" I asked.

"Illegal immigrants!"

"*What?*" I replied, incredulous.

She went on to explain how "they" flew in cargo compartments, then jumped out before "they" hit Heathrow, to avoid customs. I thought about pointing out how xenophobic—not to mention impossible—that sounded, when I remembered it was Rose who sent Christmas cards to our family's Peruvian housekeeper, not me. Rose who kept up with my family's Jamaican baby nurse from decades earlier, urging me to call her when she got sick, reminding me of her name and other details. I could learn more about the values I claimed to espouse from her actions than I could ever teach with my words.

"See?" my mom whispered a few moments later, while Rose's gaze was still transfixed on the grass patch. "She's insane!"

In my thirties, I moved to Nashville. Oddly enough, Rose had taken a summer nannying job with a family in town. Some Fridays after she'd finished work I'd pick her up. We went honky-tonkin' on Broadway. For margaritas at my favorite Mexican restaurant. We even went to see Billy Ray Cyrus at the Grand Ole Opry. Per her request, I took pictures of her in front of everything: an oversize cowboy boot. A sign that said something she thought was stupid. Lasciviously dressed mannequins. A picture she didn't ask me to take, of her taking a picture of some geese crossing a parking lot.

One time, Rose asked to sleep over after. She needed some real time off, she said. I wasn't her job anymore. I wasn't her home either. I was just me. She was just her. I drifted off to sleep that night, the low chirp of her voice in the other room, cooing softly on the phone with Phil at her midnight and his morning.

LITTLE LOLITA OF
WEST FOURTH STREET

You know the difference between you and your sisters?"
Ray asked.

He sat down on the couch next to me, then slid a
Heineken in my direction across the coffee table. Next he
opened one for himself. Apparently, he'd relapsed.

"What?" I replied, only half curious and chewing a hang-
nail. Besides, the Skynyrd *Behind the Music* was on VH1,
and I knew the answer anyway: I was accommodating. They
weren't. Big whoop.

"You're virginal," he announced in his thick Northern
accent, sounding like a pervy Beatle. I rolled my eyes: duh,
I was a virgin. I was thirteen. I nudged the beer away with
my foot, careful not to knock it over. He might want it
later.

Ray had played guitar in a semi-successful '90s rock
band. A few years earlier, when his band was still together,

my mom had picked me up from school to attend their sound check at a historic New York venue.

"Dance," she whispered after a song or two.

"What?" I asked, confused.

"You have to dance. To show them you like it."

Since my mother had married a rock star, I assumed she knew the protocol. Floating to the center of the empty floor, still sticky from stale beer, I did my best Penny Lane, spinning in circles until I grew dizzy. When I looked back for approval and permission to stop, I saw she wasn't paying attention. I kept going in case she did.

When the band split up, Ray passed a brief stint as my manny. Having a down-and-out rocker in this position wasn't unusual for my family. We'd had a few characters fill in for Rose in her offseason. There was Marley, the sexy premed student. Rob, a professional magician. While Ray couldn't hold a candle to a man who could levitate napkins and disappear watches, he was at least very funny, preferring to be recognized as my bodyguard instead of my babysitter. At a diner once, his impression of assassinating murderous waiters made Bea laugh so hard milk came through her nose, which made me laugh so hard I almost puked. When he eventually moved in with us a few months later, I didn't think much about it. We'd always had randos live with us: a ballerina from Cuba and her young son. A woman my mother saw jogging topless on the beach in Tulum. A psychic who told me I was both an alcoholic monk and a gay sailor in a past life. Courtney Love. In a way, Ray's presence actually made the most sense. Like my father, he was a musician and in and out of recovery. Like my mother, he seemed to enjoy rearranging furniture. Daily, I'd come home to find her perched on a sofa and pointing in different directions while he struggled under the weight of overstuffed armchairs, dusty antique mirrors.

"There," she'd say. And there he'd go. "No. *There*." And there he'd go again.

By the time I was fifteen, G was married to his high school sweetheart and living sensibly in Brooklyn. Mino was playing the spoons across Appalachia with her lover, a one-man band she'd met on the subway, and Emi was (presumably) at college. My father, meanwhile, was between tour and treatment. My mother, at various health spas, which meant I was often home alone with Ray. Taking full advantage of this freedom, I hosted sleepovers with girlfriends every other night and smoked ceaselessly inside. Life was good, even if Ray had progressed from taking care of me and my friends to flirting with them.

One morning I awoke to find my friend Zora blushing in her underwear.

"Why are you smiling?" I asked groggily. There was no reason for such happiness. We had school that day, and it wasn't even seven a.m.

"He kissed me," she said with a stunned smile.

"What?" I replied, disturbed.

"Well," she said, her voice pitched high, "I was in the shower, and he came in, and he just . . . kissed me!" I blinked in shock. "Oh! And then he asked me where the rolling papers were."

A few weeks later, the housekeeper found Zora's oversized bra stuffed in Ray's sheets.

"What do we do?" my mother asked, cocking her head at the mass of black lace before us, as if choosing a paint color.

"Probably give it back?" I suggested.

"You're right. It *does* look expensive," she agreed.

Unsettling as the situation was, part of me was grateful my mom didn't kick Ray out. His mirth was a welcome change, even if it was a bit much sometimes. Like one afternoon, when I was suffering through a tenth-grade English paper on *Lolita*—a complicated book but one I couldn't help feeling connected to. Maybe it was because all the Colombian seamstresses who worked in my mother's basement studio called me Lolita. Or maybe it was because I thought it was a good thing to be a sexually precocious young girl, and who was more that than Lolita?

A few Christmases earlier my mother had even gifted me an original poster of the Kubrick film version. It hung above my bed and fit right in with the rest of my childhood bedroom's decor: lust-pink walls. Nineteen thirties silk piano shawls for my bedspreads. Framed photographs of people like Brigitte Bardot, smoking.

HOW DID THEY EVER MAKE A MOVIE OF *LOLITA?* the poster asked above the iconic image of her sucking a lollipop, wearing a pair of heart-shaped sunglasses. But the real question was how was *I* supposed to write a paper about *Lolita?* Especially since by that time I was smoking so much pot, I could hardly remember five minutes ago! I struck her pose from the poster in the large silver antique vanity mirror across from me. That didn't help.

Sighing, I flipped the book open. Lolita's mom thinks she's a brat. Lolita's mom is run over by a car. Lolita secretly cries herself to sleep. Lolita just wants to be a little girl. Lolita misses her mom. Suddenly, my own mother and Ray disrupted me, laughing like hyenas three floors below. I stormed downstairs to arrest their joy but yielded when I found they weren't alone.

Gideon had been a heartthrob movie star since he was a teenager, but he no longer looked like it. In fact, he was now almost unrecognizably bearded and fat.

"It's for a role!" Ray hissed when I pulled him aside to confirm Gideon's identity.

"Well, I much preferred him young and toned."

"Well, this is a very *serious* role," Ray continued. My ears pricked up. Maybe there was a part for me. I had once been cut from a PlayStation commercial that Bob Dylan's son was directing in our house, not to mention my long list of high school theater credits.

"What is it?"

"He's playing a *grieving father*."

"Is the dead child a boy or a girl?" I asked, sensing an opening.

"Boy, I believe."

"Fuck!" I said, a little too loudly.

Gideon was sprawled across a sofa, one sneaker planted firmly on the floor while the other dirtied a couch cushion. Some confectioners' sugar from the Italian wedding cookies he was gobbling had spilled all over his T-shirt. He licked the rest from his fingers.

"I want pot," he announced to no one in particular.

"Oh, Lola *loves* pot!" replied my mother.

"No, I don't!" I lied.

My mother was staunchly anti-pot, which was problematic, since I had recently become ardently pro-it, smoking at least eight times a day. The threat of drug tests was so constant, I had taken to storing a friend's little sister's piss in mini Poland Spring bottles under my bed just in case. Fortunately, I never had to use them . . . which meant that the piss just stayed there. Anyway. After proclaiming my innocence for a few more minutes, I ran up the stairs two at a time and grabbed my stash.

"We can smoke it on the street?" I offered to Gideon privately.

"*I* can't smoke weed on the street," he replied.

"Right," I said, remembering that no matter how unsightly he currently was, he was still a famous movie star, not a teenager like me, who regularly spent her afternoons loitering on people's stoops, drinking forties, and blasting Wu-Tang from a portable speaker.

"What about if you come over?" he said.

I lied to my mother and told her I was headed to Zora's, then met back up with Gideon a few blocks later. He walked ten feet away from me the whole time. Later, I realized this was to ensure that no paparazzi shots of him walking with a teenage girl in a hot pink American Apparel catsuit materialized. At the time, I just assumed he was being rude.

"What's your favorite movie?" I yelled from a few paces behind him, trying to catch up.

"I don't watch movies!" he shouted.

"Okay," I said, disappointed. I loved movies. "What about books?"

"I don't do that either."

At his apartment, little changed. I rolled a joint on the kitchen counter, hoping he might say something complimentary about my skill. Instead, he remained silent. I searched his face, hungry for validation. His eyes followed my tongue as it licked the paper. Encouraged, I lit it and passed it, but he wouldn't take it from me.

"Put it in the ashtray," he instructed. I did. He picked it up, took a hit, then replaced it on another surface, and so on and so forth, like a little game of cat and mouse, until the joint was gone.

"Do you like music?" I asked, suddenly stoned and awkward.

"Only Elvis," he replied after a while of staring out the window.

I searched his shelf of CDs and found a greatest-hits collection. Putting it on, I wafted to the center of his loft and began to dance for him. I did a lazy twist in the middle of his living room. I wondered if my mother would be proud of me. Or if she'd kill me. Or both. Gideon watched me from the sofa through glazed-over eyes, which made it difficult to tell what impact I was having, if any. I considered what it would be like to kiss him. Or, rather, what it would be like to tell people I had. After all, not even a movie star was enough to shake my opinion about older men, which was that they should on no occasion wear sandals.

"Come sit here," he said eventually, patting his lap.

My heart twisted in my chest. My seduction had worked. I didn't like it.

"I'll just sit here instead," I said, plopping onto the sofa across from him, like the tired child I hoped he'd see I was. The sun was setting pink over the Hudson.

"I should go," I said after a minute. He didn't stop me.

A week later, I came home from school to find my mother in a foul mood.

"Where's Ray?" I asked, sensing a storm and praying he

might come to the rescue. Unfortunately, Ray was the problem. She turned her laptop around to show me an email exchange between him and Gideon. It said something about flesh and smelling it.

"I don't get it," I said.

"It's about *you*," she hissed.

Apparently, Ray had left his email open on her computer.

"It's inappropriate!" my mother squealed as I excused myself.

"Yes," I agreed. It was. But wasn't everything?

Surprisingly, when I came home from play practice a few days later, Gideon was in our kitchen.

"What are you doing here?" I asked, shocked.

"Your mother and I had a talk—"

"—and everything's fine!" She finished his sentence as she moved into the kitchen, placing a lit candelabra on the table to prepare it for dinner.

Our meal started off normal enough, but halfway through, Gideon said he felt feverish and excused himself to take an awkward nap on a nearby love seat. For a moment I wondered if my mother had poisoned him for revenge. If his breath would soon quicken, then stop altogether. Instead, he snorted and rolled over. My mother and I finished our meal in silence.

A few years after, I found myself back in Gideon's apartment with a group of older people I had met at a nightclub. When he barely said a word, I wondered if he remembered me.

"Hey," I said before mentioning my full name to jog his memory. "Ray's . . . friend?"

He was quiet for a while. I wondered if I had misspoken. A lot of people didn't like Ray anymore. He'd been banished from the city after being accused of something ugly having to do with a famous person's daughter. I feared it was true. I hoped it wasn't. Last I'd heard, he was driving Uber in L.A.

"Oh yeah," Gideon said finally. "You grew up good."

PART TWO

Bad Times, The Band, and the Big Time

Love is where you find it
When you find no love at home
And there's nothing cold as ashes
After the fire is gone.

—"After the Fire Is Gone," as sung by
Loretta Lynn and Conway Twitty

ITCHY

We all look terrible in the wedding photos. Maybe it's the unflattering purple bridesmaid dresses my sisters and I are wearing. Maybe it's the gray English sky behind us. Most likely, though, it's the black eyes and bruised limbs we're all sporting, from a fistfight we'd gotten into with each other the night before.

It was the summer between my senior year of high school and freshman year of college, and we three gals were sharing a room in London, where we'd traveled with our parents to participate in a family friend's nuptials, when the brawl erupted. You see, *Pregnant* was upset that *Tattooed** had stolen her boyfriend. Now, it wasn't the boyfriend who had gotten Pregnant pregnant—Tattooed isn't a *total* monster!— just a recent and significant ex. Understandably, Pregnant

---

* For funsies, during this segment of the story, my sisters shall be identified solely by their most defining characteristics.

was pissed. Still, I sided with Tattooed. After all, Pregnant had started it. Did she *really*, though? I mean, sure, she threw the first punch, then wished Tattooed dead, but . . . really? In any case, a few swings in, Pregnant was forcibly removed by our parents. Tattooed and I spent the rest of the night watching a *Law & Order* marathon, as if nothing had happened.

In spite of it all, the wedding was a smash. It was fairy-themed. I drank purple champagne. Kate Moss asked me where the toilet was. La-di-da. The following afternoon I woke up in a strange mansion I couldn't remember going to. From a series of Warhols, I was able to piece together that the home belonged to an iconic Texan model who'd been married to a legendary British rock star. Unsure how to leave, I sat through an awkward Sunday lunch with her and some distant cousins, all of whom believed, no matter how much I insisted otherwise, I was somehow royal. Perhaps it was the ball gown I was still wearing from the night before. When the model's gorgeous gap-toothed daughter finally awoke that evening, I was informed of an elaborate plan we'd made in the wee hours to attend a music festival. We'd be leaving shortly. Since she was the coolest person I'd ever met, I decided to skip the part where I told her I'd have to ask permission, and just go along with it. I was almost eighteen. My parents would put it together eventually.

At the festival, I saw zero bands and tried many, many drugs. Sadly, none were mind-altering enough to make me feel positively about being surrounded by swaths of shirtless Brits in the rain. I'd also misplaced all my socks and had to raw-dog it in wellies, which I don't recommend, especially if you happen to be searching for a cousin best described as "fun loving with an undercut," as apparently this counts for 75 percent of that festival's population. I never found her. A few miserable days later, when I met my dad at the festival gates, I was elated. The sun was finally out and shining right down on him calmly reading a paper in a rental car. It was a beautiful sight.

When we joined my mother at Heathrow a few hours after, I expected her usual song and dance. A tight hug. A long sniff. And then one of her two dreaded questions: "Are you high?" or "Did you have sex?"

But when I discovered her at the gate, she just pulled me close and held me in an embrace, seemingly void of ulterior motive.

"I love you, Lola," she said seriously.

"Oh, Mom," I said passionately. "Me too."

I hoped she'd never let go. It was so warm and cozy in there. Much nicer than the K-hole I'd been in for the better part of a weekend. I was relieved not to be in trouble. But my relief was quickly replaced by the sense that something was very, very wrong.

I'd spent much of my life trying to get close to Emi only to have her push me away. For a long time, I'd believed this was my fault. I was too much. Too eager. Too ugly. It never occurred to me that this could be because she felt ugly herself. From afar, I'd just glimpse the veneer of her manic-pixie-dream-girl perfection. Up close, I'd bear witness to the painstaking detail of her chaos and fury. Distance would make my heart grow fonder. Proximity might make me run for my life.

Emi needed me but feared I'd disappear unless I wanted her. Like a monster, this need mostly came out at night. Throughout elementary school, my bedroom door would creak open, to reveal the girl who wouldn't sit next to me on the subway tucking herself into the other side of my bed. She must be afraid of the dark, I reasoned. Why else would she treat nights like days and rarely sleep?

Sometimes she'd coax me into her bed with the promise of a story. Tense, I'd lie at her side as she read to me from books like *The Ballad of the Sad Café*.

"Are you listening still?" she'd ask after a paragraph or so.

"Ya."

"Okay, so what happened?" she'd test.

"She left him and now he's killing everybody."

"But why?"

"Probably because he's sad?"

"Yes. Exactly. Good," she'd say before continuing, her voice hoarse but proper, like Mary Poppins after a bender.

During her second year in college, when I was just starting high school, Emi decided I was okay, even during daylight hours. Packages began to show up for me from Providence.

Mobiles made of postcards with kind messages in her perfect script, held together by paper clips. Punk records and T-shirts. Jewelry boxes filled with plastic gems and pelts of unidentified fur. One weekend she invited me to visit her. Bringing only items that were once hers, I boarded the train to Rhode Island.

Her apartment was slanted because it was old, and cold because she'd leave the windows open so she could smoke. She had a large poster of a movie about a pretty child heroin addict, a fluffy black-and-white cat named Julian, and an antique bust of Elvis. She did a line while I smoked a cigarette. Then we went to a house party. When we arrived, she disappeared immediately. Alone, I found myself sitting on a twin bed, falling in love with a local.

Gary had sleeves of the whole solar system tattooed up and down his arms, which was fitting since, for a moment, that was what he was to me. At the end of our conversation, he punched a hole in a plywood door, then ripped a piece of it off to write his number down on.

Call me when yer [*sic*] *18,* it read above the ten digits.

When I found my sister later, I was brandishing the bit of broken door like a trophy.

"Do you know *Gary?*" I said, as if the name were somehow sexy and not evocative of a used-car salesman.

"Yeah," she replied casually. "He broke into my apartment last week."

"Oh!" I jumped, fearing I had been conned into a crush by a criminal.

"What?" she said like I was an idiot. "It was fine. We had sex."

After the party, Emi and I lay side by side in her cozy bed, soft with sheets from home. Still, I couldn't sleep. She kept shifting. Kicking. Searching for the "cold bits." She couldn't sleep either, she said. She never could.

"I could be wrong," I began slowly, sensing tender ground. "But isn't that because, like . . . coke's supposed to keep you awake?"

"Probably," she replied.

I attempted to construct a follow-up that wouldn't make me sound like Captain Obvious. It was useless.

"Then why do you do it so much?" I said finally.

There was a long pause. I feared I'd crossed a line.

"Because it's like an itch," she replied. "And each time you scratch it, it gets deeper and deeper instead of going away."

"So what if you . . . like . . . didn't scratch it then?"

I inhaled her signature musk of paint, perfume, and cigarettes, then held my breath, trying to store her somewhere within me, just in case, and forever. She said nothing.

I'd feared my sister might die since she first started using drugs in front of me when I was eleven. Having a mother who had lost her own sister to addiction, I knew second-hand how grief permanently altered the color of your life. It seemed insurmountable. The day Emi overdosed when I was in tenth grade, I began to see it also might be inevitable.

"But she's alive?" I asked my dad, who told me that afternoon when he picked me up from school.

He confirmed that she was. We called her in the hospital from the car phone.

"Hi," she peeped, sounding like a sweet English mouse, the kind Beatrix Potter might chronicle. "Can you come visit me?"

She sounded so weak. So small.

"I have too much homework," I lied.

I knew it would be best for both of us if I didn't see her like that.

A few years later, after landing in New York from London, I didn't have a choice. I had to go sit with Emi, my mom said. She was fragile after *the incident*. She couldn't be alone. Descending upon her ground-level lair, I found her greasy-haired and near catatonic.

"Hi," I said from the doorway.

She didn't acknowledge me. Maybe it was because Jordan Catalano was breaking Angela Chase's heart on TV. Or maybe it was the meds. In any case, I didn't know what to say next. My grandmother had taught me the correct way to answer "How are you?" ("I'm fine, thanks, and you?") My mother, more difficult conversational skills, like diplomacy whilst conversing with my father's mistresses. But I hadn't the slightest idea of what you were supposed to say to someone after they'd been raped by their drug dealer.

"Do you want water?" I asked.

She didn't answer. I brought her some anyway. She chugged it. I noticed her hospital bracelet still on her wrist. I thought about her undergoing tests in a backless gown. I hated it. When it seemed she'd fallen asleep, I got up to leave.

"Where are you going?" she said before I could reach the door.

"Nowhere," I replied. I sat back down.

A few days later, she asked if I'd attend a twelve-step meeting with her. I said I would then smoked a massive joint, only to realize the error of my ways once we got there. I couldn't hide how high I was. I kept slow-clapping extensively after each share, sometimes even cheering a little.

"You can't be stoned at a fucking NA meeting," Emi hissed at me after.

We were at a diner nearby and I was ripping apart a chicken tender. "Sorry," I said with my mouth full.

Cecil, an older man who lived on the streets and had also been present, agreed. "Listen to your sister," he said as he shoved some crackers in his pants.

"But what if I'm not a drug addict?"

They looked at me like addicts always do: *Of course you are.*

We spent the rest of the summer going to more meetings like this, except I didn't get high before, just after. Emi got a job working at a fish-and-chips shop around the corner from our house. She went to bed early. I was so proud of her.

One evening I found her reading a little book of poetry in the kitchen. I stood back, taking in the serene sight. It was so peaceful. So normal.

"Hi!" she chirped eventually, sensing my presence. As I opened the fridge to retrieve the chocolate-covered biscuits I stored in there when my mom was away, as she was that night, Emi smiled at me. And kept smiling. Something was off.

"I just want you to know," she began as I braced myself, "I drink wine on the sly." She revealed a small cup she'd hidden under the table.

"Oh!" I exhaled, relieved. "Well, that's fine, right? 'Cause wine's not drugs?"

"Yeah!" She laughed, so I did too. I went upstairs and ate the whole box of biscuits.

In the kitchen again a few nights later, I was surprised to discover a strange man wearing Emi's bathrobe.

"Don't worry. That's just Abe," she yelled lazily from the other room.

"Oh," I said, extending my hand properly—another example of my grandmother's manners. "Nice to meet you, Abe."

He did not shake it.

"Abe's Hasidic, so he won't touch you," Emi informed me, swinging the fridge door open and going straight for my cookies. "He doesn't believe women are people."

I looked to Abe for confirmation. He looked away. But not before I noticed his lipstick. And his *payot.*

"We're experimenting," Emi explained, ashing the crumbs of one of my cookies into her hand like it was a cigarette. Then she lit a joint, which surprised me. Weed was my thing. The thing I did when she did real drugs, so I wouldn't be left out. Weed was for kids. She puffed perfect smoke rings, then passed the joint to Abe, who coughed like it might kill him.

Very early a few mornings later, the buzzer rang. And rang. And RANG. At first I didn't get it because I figured someone else would. They didn't. Stumbling out of bed, I made the long journey three flights down the stairs to the front door to discover the police.

"Is everything okay, ma'am?"

It felt strange to be called "ma'am." At seventeen, I was still technically a child. Couldn't they see that?

"You tell me!" I replied.

"Do you have a panic button?"

I yelled up the stairs for my mom. There was no answer.

"MOMMMMMMMMMMMMMMMMMMM!" I yelled

again, as despite having an intercom, screaming was my family's primary mode of communication.

"What?" peeped an oddly timid version of her voice.

"It's the police!" I heard rustling. "Put a shirt on!"

Within seconds, she was hobbling down and stinking like alcohol, which was unusual. She never drank.

"The police are asking about a panic button?"

"Emi!" she cried. "Emi has the panic button!"

"We have a panic button?!" I asked, as the cops, myself, and my mother formed a hysterical conga line that trailed to Emi's lair on our brownstone's ground floor. Her thick metal door was bolted shut. I banged against it so hard my palms hurt. My mother wailed. The police were preparing to break it down when Emi finally answered.

"What?" she said, blinking at us like we were morons.

Her lips were chapped and caked in day-old lipstick. She smelled like she always did in the mornings: sleep and formaldehyde from too many cigarettes smoked the night before.

"You pressed the panic button, ma'am," an officer explained.

"Oh," she replied in a daze. "I must have confused it for the remote."

She was alive, thank god. But she was also clearly using.

I put Emi back to bed, then sent the police away, before interrogating my mother.

"What the hell is going on with you?" I screamed.

"I—I—" she began to answer before dissolving into tears. "Your father left!"

"To go where?"

"I don't know!"

"Well," I said, trying to sound reassuring, "I'm sure he'll come back?"

"I don't know," she croaked, wiping the tears off her face like a child, using her whole arm. I caught a whiff of her. She stank like a frat boy on a Sunday morning.

"Where were you last night?" I asked, trying to get us back on track.

Through heaving sobs, she explained that a hip young movie star had taken her to a new nightclub in town, already famous for a pair of burlesque dancing twins who smoked cigarettes through their vaginas. I couldn't help but feel impressed. And jealous. I had been desperate to go to that club and unable to get in.

After tucking my mother into bed, I went into the kitchen hoping to finally start my day the way I did every day, or else the sky fall and everyone in the world die. Two soft-boiled eggs with a Portuguese muffin, lightly toasted, heavily buttered, and cut into soldiers, just like my dad used to make me. Napkin folded into a triangle. Butter knife and little spoon arranged just so nearby. As I was setting my small glass of orange juice on the far-left edge of my place mat, the buzzer rang once more. I resigned myself to answering it.

"Uh . . ." a man in khaki shorts hesitated. "Is Emi here?"

If it wasn't for his messenger bag, I probably wouldn't have put together that he was a drug dealer. If it wasn't for his anxiety, I probably wouldn't have put together that it was *the* drug dealer. The one who'd put my sister in the hospital. Stunned, I said nothing. He smiled almost apologetically, and after a moment, turned on his heel and bolted the other direction.

LAND OF THE FLOWERS

I did my best to make my half of my freshman-year dorm feel as glamorous as my bedroom back home. A foreign film poster here, a scarf over a lamp there. If I squinted, the decade-old vomit stain on the carpet added a texture that almost evoked our original hardwood floors. But once my roommate started chatting with her dad in "Western Mass" (why people from there feel so compelled to distinguish themselves from the rest of the state, I have no idea), my fantasy would be ruined. Nightly, she'd hem and haw as they discussed the merits of the Bible as compared to the Koran. Nightly, I'd rue the day I was born.

I had chosen Bard because I hadn't gotten in anywhere else. Sure, I took the SAT three times, but I never scored very high, likely because I always *was* very high. Attempting to compensate for my poor academics with my creativity, I'd decorated my application envelopes to Ivy League schools with doodles of stars, sometimes even pouring in a teaspoon of glitter. When none of this worked, I managed to talk my way into my alma mater by recounting the plot of Priscilla Presley's memoir, *Elvis and Me*, to their head of admissions and using my hands *a lot*. They let me in on the spot, a victory I celebrated by ripping a joint in the woods behind the office immediately after.

My glory was short-lived. I hated it there. All around me, others were beginning their lives while mine felt like it was ending. I longed for New York City. Or Gainesville, Florida, where my boyfriend, Ryder, had just returned after being exiled from New York City—though I wasn't exactly sure why. He had been vague about the reason, other than, as usual, everyone was always against him.

Ryder and I had started dating during my senior year of high school after meeting at a nightclub my mother had taken me to. While this wasn't the one with the twins who smoked vagina cigarettes, going there was still exciting to me, even if I already went there by myself all the time. Being underage, I'd discovered the secret to getting in wasn't having a fake ID but looking like you didn't give a shit. Instead of makeup and flattering clothes, I wore plastic sandals with socks and nightgowns. It worked every time.

The night I met Ryder, though, I'd let Emi dress me— for old times' sake. Clad in a tight-fitting blue leopard-print dress, white thigh-highs, and saddle shoes I had bought after reading *Lolita*, I looked my teenage version of irresistible. Incidentally, Ryder also looked my teenage version of irresistible, though it turned out he was actually a bit older.

After chatting for hours in the dark, Ryder and I went out front to smoke cigarettes with my mom. Fortunately, even she found him charming, a good sign, as her instincts, while annoying, were mostly right. A few hours later, we went to my house a few blocks away. Eventually, he would tell me it was the house, not me, he was impressed with. But that night, when things were just beginning, we kissed in the garden. I played him records I liked. He showed me YouTube videos of Pavement. I was in love. It was terrible. Not at first, but very soon after.

A struggling musician, Ryder was perpetually broke, drunk, and jealous—which, for a long while, was exactly my type. Who doesn't love a good project? At college the following year, I missed him like crazy. When fall break rolled around, I got my wish: a ticket to Jacksonville. And cab fare from there to Gainesville because he didn't want to come pick me up. After being kicked out of the band he had been playing with in New York, Ryder was living back on the Suwannee River with his mom, a nice nurse with a clean house that had multiple hot tubs. While this made them seem like they had money, it was really because his stepdad *sold* hot tubs. Ryder would explain this all the time, because he hated rich people.

"But I'm rich," I'd remind him.

"Yeah," he'd agree. "It's your worst quality."

After a few days spent shooting clay pigeons and checking out the neighbors' reptile collection, I managed to convince Ryder he should reconnect with his father. They'd been estranged for a few years by that point and my degree as an armchair psychologist told me this was why he was so angry all the time. When Ryder finally agreed, I was overjoyed. Perhaps I could fix him after all.

His dad was younger than I'd imagined and much taller. He shared an apartment with his girlfriend, Rory, and her adult son, Travis, both of whom worked the night shift in a hospice, which meant he often had the place to himself. A large nativity scene decorated the area around their TV, which I took to mean they were either really religious or had forgotten to take it down last year. Things were normal enough though. We watched *Legends of the Fall* in recliners and drank beer. A few hours and a case of Busch Light later, Ryder and his father seemed unaffected by whatever conflict had driven them apart. In fact, I'd never seen Ryder so happy. I felt proud to have brought about their reunion. But I was also starting to wonder how we were going to get out of there if Ryder kept drinking. After all, he was the driver. *I* was from New York City.

When the sun set, I asked Ryder quietly if we could possibly go soon. In response, he fell over. I took that as a no. Ryder and his dad shotgunned more beers, which they spilled all over the carpet. I decided to give them some space and put myself to sleep in Ryder's dad and girlfriend's bed. When I got up to pee around three a.m., father and son were still at it, using a jimmied paper clip to scrape resin out of a pipe and watching YouTube. When morning finally came, I was relieved. Ryder was next to me, drooling, a blue hue coloring just below his nostrils.

"Wake the fuck up," I said as sweetly as possible. He didn't like it when I had a tone with him.

Just then, the bedroom door swung open to reveal Ryder's dad's girlfriend, home from her shift.

Rory was older than Ryder's dad. Pushing sixty, she wore Daisy Dukes and a pair of platform flip-flops. Her skin was orange, and her hair was cropped and bright blond. She held a White Russian in each hand and climbed into bed between Ryder and me to hand them to us.

"Good morning, sunshines!" she croaked.

I prayed Ryder wouldn't drink the White Russian, fearing that if he did, he would drink five more, and we'd be trapped for another day. He chugged it.

In the living room, Rory's son, Travis, sat in a La-Z-Boy across from Ryder's dad, who didn't appear to have moved from his recliner since I last saw him. Neither said much. Travis rolled a blunt. Rory mixed more White Russians.

"Oh, Ryder!" she lilted. "Do you remember Gina from my old apartment building?"

"Who?"

"Gina—with the twins?"

"What about her?"

"She's dead! She fell down the stairs, and nobody found her *for days*."

Like my mother, Rory seemed to have a passion for sharing devastating news. I found this mildly comforting. Ryder did not. He chugged another White Russian. When he put the glass down, he had a white milk mustache, which complemented the blue dusting beneath his nose nicely.

"Ooo! Ooo!" Rory continued. "And remember her boyfriend, Desmond?"

He didn't say anything.

"You'll *never* believe what happened to him," she carried on. "*He* shot himself!"

I kicked Ryder under the table to try to covertly communicate that we had to leave.

"Why are you kicking me?!" he shrieked.

Rory told more stories, each ending with someone else she knew dying. Travis lit the blunt. Smoke filled the room.

Later that afternoon, Ryder was lying on a picnic table in the backyard with his shirt off and draped across his eyes.

"Ryder," I said firmly, "I really want to leave."

Just then, my phone started ringing. It was my mother. While I would have done anything for her in that moment, I was too afraid to answer. I didn't want to get into trouble. She would hate hearing I was in a place with so many La-Z-

Boys. I let it go to voicemail. A moment later, she was calling again. I wondered if this meant my sister was dead.

"Hello?" I answered.

"Lola!" she said, sounding unusually pleased. "Well, Emi just came to me. And she said, 'Mummy, I want to go to rehab.' So, she's going! YAY!"

I started to cry. She mistook my tears for joy.

"I know!" she replied. "Isn't it wonderful?"

"Yes. I'm just . . . so happy," I said, wishing I was. But I wasn't. I was angry. Nothing I ever did was bad enough to make anyone care this much. Nothing I ever did was good enough to make them change.

When I hung up, Ryder asked what was wrong with me.

"My . . . my sister's going to rehab," I said as pathetically as possible, hoping he'd take pity on me and we could finally go.

"Why is everyone in your family always going to rehab?"

I considered explaining that, from my understanding, everyone seemed to struggle with voids in their lives they were attempting to fill with substances, but this seemed lost on a man who'd drunk six White Russians for breakfast.

Ryder drove twenty miles an hour the whole way back to his mom's house, scared that if he went faster, he'd be arrested. I left the next day. I needed to be there for my sister and my family. Even if I was left to wonder: who was going to be there for me?

CLEMENTINE

Besides not getting in anywhere else, the main reason I had "chosen" my school was for its robust rock-and-roll folklore. The Vandals allegedly took *those* handles at *that there* gas station! Steely Dan was never coming back to *this* old school! Most alluring of all were the whispers that the Band had once used the campus as a place to score chicks. Over the last few years, the classic rock outfit had swiftly usurped the Strokes' throne in my heart. Secretly, I harbored the magical thought that soon I'd be grown up enough to both meet and party with my idols. I had not considered then that time stops for no one: as I got older, so too did they. There would always be gaps between me and the people I loved so much it hurt.

Nostalgia for something you've never experienced can yield untenable melancholy. I was forty years too late and depressed as hell about it. But when I learned the Band's drummer, Levon Helm, was not only alive but well and just across the river, playing concerts in his home every Saturday night, my hope was restored. Soon enough, a local taxi was transporting me through the dead of winter, down Tinker Street, up the driveway to Levon's house, and back in time. When I arrived, I discovered my version of heaven: a group of (retired) Hells Angels content in their new lives as Levon's security detail, a blazing fire pit swarmed by fans from near and far. Sure, everyone was a little wrinklier than I had imagined, but there was a whole table of homemade pies that were FREE. And then there was Ophelia! And Evangeline! Could I stay? They needed valet parkers! I could do that! But could I drive? No!

Crossing the bridge over the Hudson on the cab ride back to campus that night, I looked up to see the sky wide and starless with January cold. I felt almost comforted by the signs bolted to the sides of the bridge, making sure people didn't jump. YOU ARE NOT ALONE! they promised.

But I was. Until I met Ada.

Unlike the fast-living kids I knew from New York City who wore leather jackets and Air Force 1s, Ada, a fifth-generation Californian, wore tattered prairie dresses and boots that made it look like she'd been hiking but in the '70s. She always had a dog-eared copy of *Trout Fishing in America* in her backpack, which, if I'm remembering correctly, was a burlap sack. She wore her hair pin-straight and parted down the middle, drove stick, and spoke the easy way free-spirited girls in old movies did. She had the coloring of a beautiful coyote, and the daring too: she'd once been apprehended for a form of breaking and entering. I'd never met anyone so brave.

Immediately, I reoriented my entire life to be just like her. I traded in my Camel Filters for her American Spirits, my skinny jeans for her Levi 501s. My drink order became Wild Turkey 101 *neat*, because that was what she drank. I copied her incense (piñon) and her scent (patchouli) and even hoped to achieve some of her effect on others too: while I struggled to get Ryder to write a single song about me, she was constantly enraged by how many of her lovers made her into characters in their concept albums and novels. She was tired of being a muse . . . which made me scared she'd realize that she was in fact my muse. But she mustn't have noticed, or cared really, because one day she suggested we start a band ourselves.

We'd go by our shared middle name, Clementine, and outfit ourselves in her clothes. As for the instrumentation, a man in San Francisco had once given her a mandolin to leave his apartment, and like many white girls in the mid-2000s, I sort of played the ukulele.

My dad had gifted me one for my seventeenth birthday. Subsequently, instead of actually attending school, I spent most of my senior year sitting outside the building, strumming my favorite tunes out of *Jumpin' Jim's Ukulele Songbook: Country*. Fortunately, my truancy was of no concern to the faculty, in particular my calculus teacher, who told us that if we wanted to skip class we could, as long as we were *honest* about why. One afternoon, when he passed me on the steps after I'd missed yet another lesson, I decided to put his rule to the test.

"Hello, Mr. Lockwood!" I waved.

"Howdy, Lola."

"I didn't come to class today because I wanted to learn 'Crazy' by Patsy Cline."

"That's wonderful, Lola. I hope you enjoyed yourself!"

"I did! Would you like to hear it?" I asked hopefully.

"No!" He smiled. The honesty went both ways.

Despite not always winning me friends and influencing people, my ukulele became a sort of security blanket. I took it everywhere and sang for anyone who'd listen. The instrument brought me so much joy that when it came time to visit Emi at rehab, I asked if she'd like me to bring her one too.

"I guess," she said, as a fantasy of our world-famous folk duo filled my head. The next day, I forked over hard-earned babysitting money for a uke painted like a pineapple. When I gave it to Emi a few weeks later, she seemed genuinely thrilled, which shocked me. Treatment, I supposed, was changing her.

"Look what my sister brought me!" She beamed at her roommate, Lacey, a woman with cropped red hair and a trache she'd sustained after surviving decapitation from a drunk-driving accident.

Lacey pressed her fingers to her neck to speak. "Cute," she said in her robot voice.

I was proud. Maybe my hunch was real. Maybe music would finally bring us together.

During that visit to Emi's rehab, the two of us smoked cigarettes on the swing set, kicking our legs as we did to swing higher over the Tucson Mountains. Her skin was bright, and her eyes were clear. We held hands. She showed me off to her friends: a Louisiana woman with a voice like Reba's who liked pills, a handsome boy from Michigan who carved angry words into his arms. When a famous movie star allegedly checked in one afternoon, we whisper-guessed at who it might be.

"You finally have your sister back," my mother said to me in the cafeteria one morning, beaming at our blossoming relationship. I smiled, though I disagreed. I'd never had her before.

When the last day rolled around, we had to sit in a circle and make "amends" for our past behavior, which is rehab for say-sorry-but-mean-it.

"I'm really sorry that I was high when I went with you to your first NA meeting," I admitted, feeling like the worst person in the world.

"It's okay," Emi said.

"Good job," a counselor said.

"You can heal now," said another, patting me on the back.

Next it was Emi's turn. I kicked back, confident as a spoiled kid on Christmas: I was getting *a lot*. And it was gonna be *good*.

"Lola," she said, exhaling. "I'm sorry that I kissed your first love."

I waited for her to say *on the penis*. But when my father began a slow clap, I realized that was it.

"Good girl, Emi," he said, tears of joy welling in his eyes as tears of rage formed in mine.

How were we going to be two halves of a world-famous folk duo if she couldn't tell me the whole truth?

Ada would make a fabulous replacement, even if neither of us could really play our instruments. But that was no matter! We'd heard country was just "three chords and the truth." Since that seemed manageable enough, we decided to focus on the genre exclusively. Plus after all the lies I'd been told, I liked the honesty policy.

We went to work right away, printing out lyrics to our favorite country songs at the school library, singing them huskily because we both smoked so much. Soon it was time for our first concert, incidentally a stadium show, in that it took place in our school's empty soccer stadium. We sang in unison, not harmony. We looked fucking fantastic. At least that's what the two people in attendance said.

We pushed on, writing songs of our own, making T-shirts, trying and failing to harmonize. As with many bands, eventually our personal relationship began to suffer. I no longer liked myself around Ada. Or maybe I just realized I didn't have a self around her.

Ada was free in a way I would never be. Free to drink too much or sleep with the wrong person and not care about it; unlike me, who always hated myself when I did those things. She held herself to a lower standard but set a higher bar. Her imperfection made her perfect. She looked it too. Like Emi, Ada had the power to make me feel badly dressed in even my best outfit. She not only replaced Emi in my band but in my psyche too. I hadn't stepped out of my sister's shadow. I'd redrawn it around someone else. We played one more concert. Then we broke up.

A few months later, Ada came to me, insisting we exploit a spur-of-the-moment press opportunity. A fancy magazine was doing a piece on our school and had selected a small number of students to represent it, including our old band, Clementine.

"It's good exposure! *And* it's a country-music magazine!"

"It's *Town and Country*, Ada!"

"All publicity is good publicity!"

"But we're not even together anymore!"

Suddenly, she looked as if she might cry. Though we were the same age, I had always viewed Ada as an elder impervious to my rejection, instead of a peer, as hungry for my approval as I was hers. My desire for a big sister who took an interest in me was so desperate, I hadn't noticed the obvious truth: Ada was just another lonely kid in search of a home that might cherish her more than the one she had come from.

"Fine," she said. "I'll do it alone."

One of the most famous photos of the Band, taken by Elliott Landy, renders the five of them in sepia tones, standing in a line before the majestic Catskill Mountains and dressed in their usual 1960s-does-1860s costume. The Band allude to this era of history in several of their biggest songs, including the now controversial "The Night They Drove Old Dixie Down," which chronicles the life of a Confederate soldier in the wake of the Civil War. It was their uncanny ability to subvert narratives about the American South into their music that cemented them as one of the preeminent acts in Americana—a fact that might seem strange to sticklers who will remark that they, for the most part, were Canadian.

Sometimes I like to think that the Band, like me or Ada, were a bunch of out of place kids who fantasized that life might suit them better somewhere they could never go. I hear it in the longing of Richard Manuel's voice and piano.

The faux confidence in Rick Danko's swagger. Robbie Robertson's ambitious guitar. Garth Hudson's meandering organ—as if the more notes he plays, the more likely someone is to finally hear him. To me, the Band ooze a desire to belong to something. How else do you explain four Canadian boys latching on to one Southern man and whittling his Americanness into their own identity?

The day of the shoot it rained. In the photo, Ada and I are sheltering under a tree, holding our instruments and pretending to play. She's dressed like an authentic pioneer woman. I'm dressed like I tried to dress like a pioneer woman but got it wrong. I'm looking at her, as if awaiting instruction. She's looking away from me, the direction she was headed.

MURPHY'S LAW

I am not a child of divorce but I am an adult of one. As a child, I actually *hoped* my parents would get divorced for reasons that should be obvious by now. Not to mention I would have gotten two bedrooms, two computers, and whatever else it was one didn't allow to spite the other. When it did happen, however, I was blindsided.

It was the December after I'd graduated college. My childhood best friend, Mona, and I were doing Christmas with my parents in Miami, where they'd gotten an apartment for snowbirding purposes. Typically, I just used their place as a crash pad during Art Basel, while I waited to score invitations to glamorous parties that never came. That holiday season, I was there to tan and ensure that Mona got her very first lap dance at one of SoBe's finest strip clubs, carrying on a tradition Emi had started with me. Besides, my parents were fighting like cats and dogs. What else were us gals to do before New Year's Eve rolled around and we were finally back to New York and our independence?

Determined to find a better bar than the terrifying full nude one where they served only nonalcoholic chardonnay and the strippers believed Emi and me to be lovers, Mona and I combed one seedy club after another. But our mission was impossible. After midnight, we settled on a sad club the size of a shoebox. Women with C-section scars and underwear like you might wear on your period danced on the tiny bar. We couldn't drink enough before we decided to call it.

A couple hours later, my parents woke us for our flight. Even though I'd wanted the trip to end since it had begun, when it finally came to leaving, I was depressed. On the drive to the airport the distressed mother and clueless father I'd resented the entire time had tenderized. For a moment they were their best selves—the ones who redeemed all other qualities and made me proud to be who I was. The ones I thought might actually love each other. Then we realized my dad had driven us to Fort Lauderdale, not Miami Airport, which was an hour in the other direction.

"Ah!" my father declared as we hightailed it thirty miles back. "Murphy's Law!"

I expected my mother to chastise him as she usually did. Instead, she laughed and reached her soft hand behind the passenger seat into mine in the back seat. Back in Miami, I tried to rush through our parting embraces so I could make my flight. When my dad hugged me, he wouldn't let go.

When I finally pulled away, his eyes were misty. I tried not to make much of it. He always cried when I left. On my own afterward, I would too.

I loved my dad, even if I often felt like a fool for doing so. There were of course the shocks. The sad surprises. Still, I loved his breakfasts and the feel of his calloused fingertips from playing guitar so long. I loved his thin blond hair and his spectacles and sweaters. I loved the cheap hair gel he used and how he never rubbed his sunscreen fully in. I loved the way he'd demonstrate musical things by saying "boom gat a boom boom gat" and told the same stories over and over. I loved the long corny notes he left me when I'd do big things like finish school or star in plays. I loved how charming everyone found him and how I felt some of his charm had rubbed off on me too. I loved his mother. I loved how he never got angry at me. I loved how he drove me everywhere no matter what time, even if sometimes he drove the wrong direction.

And I loved my mom too. I loved how bad she was at telling stories because she got too excited to finish the sentence that led to the one you really needed to hear to actually understand the point of it. Her dark humor and bright colors. Her bathtubs in bedrooms. Her bedrooms in gardens. Her warm body. Her cozy sheets. Her ferocity. Her loyalty. Her rebelliousness. Her perfume, the name of which in French translated to "a brawl or a scuffle." I'd even grown to love some of the things I'd once abhorred: her messy hand-writing, her emphasis on the manners of others and failure to have many of her own. I loved her tears at funny movies. Her laughter, loud and random, as if she were the child I sometimes saw her as—the pudgy, Sephardic-looking one I'd seen in faded photos, who felt less than her fair-haired sisters. I loved her love, even if some days I felt smothered by it.

What I hated was how my parents were together. At least I thought I did, until I never saw them together again.

After rushing through security, I realized I'd forgotten to close my tab at the nudie bar the night before. I considered canceling my credit card altogether before saying fuck it and calling my dad to ask if he'd pick it up. He assured me he would. I felt lucky to have a dad who'd made so many mistakes. It meant he didn't judge me when I made them myself.

The following morning, on New Year's Day, I awoke to a text.

> Hello Darling—
> Got your credit card. Will mail it to you.

I replied that he didn't have to mail it, that he could just give it to me when he was back in New York in a few days. He wrote:

Mum and I are getting a divorce. Not sure when I'll
see you next.
xx Daddy

I didn't see him for almost two years.

Sometimes I like to think my dad drove an hour in the
wrong direction that day on purpose. A few more moments
together in the car, as a father, as a daughter, as a family.
He hasn't driven me anywhere since. But that's okay. I don't
need him to anymore. I can drive myself now.

BLADES OF GRASS

I have been fired twice. The first was during my stint as a junior counselor at a camp on Long Island where, instead of doing any actual work, I spent hours glimpsing myself in the bathroom mirror, trying to decide exactly how beautiful I was. So I suppose I deserved it. The other one not so much.

When I was twenty-two and about a year into my acting career, my agents had me fly out to Los Angeles for one screen test and another audition. Both were for big books being adapted into bigger movies.

"Which?" my mom asked, her mouth barely opening, as if to preserve energy for a more worthy endeavor.

"Well, one's about a somewhat mousy girl who moves into a handsome billionaire's sex dungeon," I recounted excitedly.

"Yeah. I read that one. And?"

"And the other is about this woman who fakes her own murder and blames it on her—"

"OOOO! I LOVE THAT ONE WHO ARE YOU? The main girl?"

"Well, no—"

"Oooo, I know, the one with the great breasts who's *so* beautiful?"

That didn't ring a bell, but I hadn't read the script yet because there wasn't one. "Uh, maybe? Is that character's name Greta?"

She moved her head an inch to help her think, invested now. "No . . . Greta . . . Greta . . ." she mused. "Not *Greta!*" she commanded, disappointed.

"What?" I cocked my head, innocent.

"She's slutty trailer trash!"

A few days later, I was in the middle seat of the last row of a 747, memorizing the "dummy sides"* for my audition. As I committed the sex dungeon scene to memory, I began to recognize it as a monologue from a very intense Swedish film. In it, the heroine details getting fucked on a beach by two teenage boys. This hit close to home. Not because I had actually done this, but because, after watching it, I thought if I were going to be famous, I should at least have the *option* and dumped my first true love, a sunflower of a man from San Francisco named Daniel, just in case.

---

* What they call an audition scene for a movie that has no script yet, either because they can't be bothered to write one or because it's so high-profile they can't send it out to us dummies they call actors.

Hollywood-bound a few days later, I realized my mistake: I *never* wanted to do MMF. In fact, I found threesomes in general to be rather boring and had spent the couple I'd attended on the sidelines, smoking. I missed Daniel terribly. So inconsolable was I that I sobbed all the way through the rest of the flight, all the way to the studio, and all the way through the audition. Apparently, my weepy approach was such a unique take on the role that I was asked to return the next day and do it all over again for the executives. In the interim, I called Daniel and begged him to take me back. He acquiesced. At my callback, I was so happy I couldn't eke out a single tear. Oh well!

Next came my audition for what my mother had deemed "slutty trailer-trash girl." I brought a bag of Skittles with me because I had heard that eating made acting, like so many things, easier. Unfortunately, I hadn't yet practiced doing them both at the same time. When the casting director rolled the camera, I went to open the bag and spilled them all over the floor. Instead of stopping, I decided to do the scene while eating the candy off the ground. Next thing I knew, I was in a makeup chair in Missouri, getting a cold sore painted onto my lip.

I had a few scenes where I chain-smoked and ate more candy and burped. I took my mother to the premiere at a fancy film festival in New York. Even though I wasn't the girl she'd wanted me to be, she was still very proud. I wore her dress and shoes and got a blowout. I felt like a star. I broke up with Daniel again and for good.

A few weeks later, I got a call. An up-and-coming director wanted to meet with me about being the lead in her new film based on my performance in the other one. She was staying at a small apartment in Murray Hill, hiding out after an exhausting press tour for her most recent movie, an indie darling. We went out for beers to woo each other, making ourselves sound as interesting as possible. I talked about my love of Elvis (borrowed from my sister, though, sure, I liked him too) and Altman films (I'd only seen one at that point, but whatever, I wanted the job). She detailed her obsession with the *Back to the Future* franchise. I lied and pretended I'd seen them all.

"We should hang out again," she said intently.

"Yes! When?"

"Tomorrow. Like eleven a.m.?"

That seemed soon.

"Sure!" I agreed.

The next morning, we met at a karaoke bar in my neighborhood. She filmed me as I sang her favorite songs from the '80s. Apparently, music featured heavily in her new script, which I was beginning to understand was about a character very much like the one I had just played, except she was missing an arm and a leg and lived in a futuristic desert world she navigated on her stomach by skateboard. A plum role, to say the least. After a few whiskeys, we went back to my apartment, where she grew very intense.

"I feel like we're about to fuck—"

"Oh!" I exclaimed.

"Not literally! I'm very straight. I mean *artistically.*"

"Oh. Okay," I replied, trying to act like I knew where she was going with this.

"But the producers are standing in our way. They won't let me cast you just yet and we need to start rehearsing. Immediately. This is a very serious part."

"So what do we do?" I panicked.

"I think you should buy a plane ticket and come to Los Angeles. You can sleep on my couch."

A week later, our rehearsals began and saw me doing things like:

- Parading down Venice Beach in a pair of hot pants I bought, with BAD BITCH airbrushed across the butt, as she filmed.
- Trying on lingerie at a racy boutique. She filmed this as well.
- Skating down her suburban West Hollywood street ass-naked. She filmed again.

I had never felt so important.

At night, we drank red wine and chain-smoked and

watched movies. After a few bottles, she'd inevitably start throwing things at the TV. By the fourth night, I was beginning to feel a little suffocated. Her couch was leather and made noises when I'd toss in my drunken slumbers. Her beautiful house was a total mess. I'd decided I'd clean up a little, a gesture of my gratitude, when she told me to get in the car. We were going north, to meet her parents.

Though it should have been obvious from her general demeanor that, like me, she had grown up wealthy, I somehow hadn't put that together. The house was sterile, the way most situated on golf courses are. An infinity pool crested over a mountainous vista. Matching antiques abounded. As soon as we walked inside, the director began yelling for her mother like a hungry child, leaving me alone to wander the home's vast expanses.

Eventually, she reemerged, angry, with a gun in her hand. "Outside. Now!" she commanded.

I obeyed.

Fortunately, she wasn't going to shoot me—she just wanted her father to teach me how to use a gun because, apparently my character was an expert. We fired bullets into a perfect blue California sky, toward lesser homes in the valley below.

Back in the car on the road to L.A., my phone rang. It was my agent, calling with some troubling news about the film.

"They're not gonna pay you for rehearsal," she said.

"Okay. That's fine."

"And they're not gonna reimburse you for any of your travel."

"Never mind that! It's for the sake of art!"

"And they want you to pay for your own lodging in the desert where they're shooting."

The deal only seemed to be getting worse. Whatever. I was determined to take a stand for the project.

"Listen, Lola, I know you love this movie, but something smells off here."

Suddenly, the car flooded with the stench of shit. We were on that part of the 5 where all the cows are. I wondered if this was a sign but decided, if it was, to ignore it. After all, the role had at least two out of three of the makings of an Oscar win: missing limbs and a Southern accent. I was determined to play it.

"I wanna do whatever is best for this movie. I don't care about money!" I said, with the confidence of someone who had never had to worry about their finances. When I hung up, I looked toward the director, in search of approval. I didn't get any. We drove the rest of the way in silence.

In the morning, the director woke me earlier than usual.

"Get up," she commanded, snapping open the blinds.

Confusingly, she was wrapped in a string of Christmas lights.

"I never, NEVER wanna hear you talk business EVER again."

"What are you talk— Oh, you mean yesterday? In the car? That was me saying how much I *don't care about business* 'cause we're making *art!*"

"Look"—she stepped toward me forcefully—"*agents* are like blades of grass. And *my movies* are like bubbles—"

"Haven't you only really made one movie?"

"Shut up! Do you know what happens to bubbles when they fall on blades of grass?"

I pictured a beautiful soap bubble floating in a field. For a moment I felt peace.

"They burst!" she continued. "They fucking burst. So when I heard you having that fucking call with your fucking bubble-burster yesterday, do you know what happened to me? I lost my fucking boner!"

"Look, I am *so* sorry. I'd never want to impact your . . . boner . . . but please believe me when I say I would do anything to be in your movie. I swear."

She looked at me dubiously. "Really? *Anything?* Because you haven't even started practicing your walk yet."

She was right. I hadn't worked on my amputee walk yet. At all. I was starting to get up so I could begin when she stopped me.

"Where are you going?"

"To practice!"

"Not now you aren't," she said, slamming the wall behind her with her hand for emphasis.

I was stunned. And still confused about the Christmas lights. "Why are you wearing those?" I asked timidly.

"Because I'm gonna act out the movie from start to fin-ish," she said, plugging herself into the wall. She glowed. *"With music."*

In hindsight, I find it odd that even after watching her move around her living room, to the extent the string of lights would allow, talking to herself and yelling at her sound system, I didn't question anything. After all, she was an important artist. Having grown up around them, I'd learned well: important artists can do whatever the fuck they want. I spent the rest of the afternoon practicing my amputee walk, hoping one day I might finally be an im-portant artist too.

Back in New York, my agent called with more bad news.

"They're firing you."

"Was it my walk? I swear I've been practicing!" I pleaded.

"They wouldn't say. And they've asked that you refrain from contacting her. She's deep in her creative process and doesn't welcome distractions . . . something about blades of grass and bubbles. I don't know, Lola. I'm sorry."

I deliberated whether to ask my next question, even though I knew the answer might break my heart. "Do they have someone else already?"

My agent exhaled. "Yes."

"Who? Who!"

When she told me, I was surprised. It was a girl who had been in the tabloids recently for dating a famous actor. I didn't know she was an actress too.

A few months later, I was back in Los Angeles, working on something else when my mom came to visit. She was staying at a classic hotel in Hollywood where we met for dinner.

"How's the room?" I asked.

"Terrible. It looks like an alcoholic screenwriter shot himself there in the forties and all they did was clean up the blood, but you wouldn't know that from the price."

Like me, my mother had great disdain for L.A.

"But you know what! I've met the loveliest girl. We use the treadmills together. She's very fit. Though she has this terrible limp, poor thing—I don't know how she does it."

"Cool," I said, dragging three french fries through some ketchup in silent protest, then through some mayonnaise to seal the deal, before stuffing them into my mouth.

"Ooo! There she is!"

When I looked up, I realized my mother's new friend was the girl from the tabloids, my replacement. She waved enthusiastically with one hand, while the other remained dutifully pinned behind her back. She began to hobble over, her smile wide, until she saw me.

"Oh!" she demurred.

"Hi," I offered, a little embarrassed. We both knew I'd been fired from her current role.

"So what do I do in the movie? I don't even act!"

I was charmed by her self-awareness. "I'm sure you'll be just fine."

She kissed my mother on both cheeks, then bobbed back to her table.

For a second I felt a little bad for her. A beautiful girl with such a bad limp. Then I remembered: she was just acting. I felt guilty for underestimating her. I hoped she wouldn't continue to underestimate herself. I hoped the movie would be a flop.

ROCK LEGEND

I always dreamed of having a younger sibling. When I was sixteen, I found out I had one.

It is the end of winter break and thank God. My parents have spent our entire trip to Brazil fighting. At the Rio airport, waiting for the flight home, things are no different. We are at the gate, and my mom is yelling at my dad so loudly I can hear her over the Bose noise-canceling headphones they got me for Christmas *and* I have them turned up all the way. I watch my father ignore her as she whirls around him in a wild rage. I don't think too much of it. Fighting like this is almost ritualistic for them. Their strange mating dance.

Eventually, my mom gives up on him and starts toward me. *If I keep my headphones on*, I think, *she will go away*, like someone on the street begging for money. But she doesn't. She just keeps talking. I take an ear out. She is very upset. I ask her why.

"They're suing again!" she yells.

"Who?"

"Your brother," she replies, as if this should be obvious.

"G?" I ask, confused as to why G would sue us. He is by far the least dramatic out of all of us—the only problem he has ever caused that he's never caused one.

"No!" she says. "Your *other* brother."

I don't know what she is talking about, which I tell her, so she tells me: my father has a son with another woman I've never heard about. Today she is upset because the other woman is suing for more child support.

"We'll have to sell the house!" she sobs.

But I am still stuck on the bit about my having a brother I've never heard of.

"What's his name?" I ask, stunned.

She ignores me. This is not the conversation she wants to have. She just wants to vent. I almost don't blame her. It's a lot.

"You'll have to switch schools!" she continues.

"Where is he?"

"I don't know. Somewhere. Phoenix!"

"How long have you known about him?"

"Since he was born!"

"When was that?"

"I don't know. Ten years ago!"

"What's his name?" I ask again.

My mom yells my dad's name so loudly he turns around. I am confused.

"*She named him after your father,*" she says, shaking her head, the insult to her injury.

I spend the eleven-hour flight home crying inside a scarf I also got for Christmas. It is red and black with skulls and tough like I want to be. It is very itchy on my wet face, which surprises me because it's good cashmere.

I picture my little brother cute and very funny. In my fantasy, I show him cool music. We have pretend fights about how the Who are inferior to the Stones. We are best friends even though I tell everyone I hate him. We're both too old to, but we still suck our thumbs.

A couple months later, to prove to myself I am a good person, I have used the part of my allowance I don't spend on weed to sponsor Nondumisu, a little girl in Africa, through a Christian organization. They are supposed to send me monthly updates like her school photos and drawings, but I forgot to send a check in January, and let that be a lesson to me because my mom is always saying how important it is that I learn to put checks in envelopes and now it's April and I'm scared Nondumisu is dead. A casualty of my negligence. Junk, junk, junk. A rejection letter from Oberlin. Oh well. Not a peep from Nondumisu. Bills. A very late Christmas card for Dad, marked numerous times "return to sender."

Since my family isn't really friends with people who send Christmas cards, I imagine it's just from a fan or something. My dad likes to become friends with his fans, and they like to send him things. Sometimes his fans are very rich men his own age who can't play music themselves but have enough money to keep people around them who do. Sometimes they are attractive women. Either way, my mother hates them. She doesn't like it anymore that my dad is a rock star. His gold records are piled in stacks in the subbasement. Rock and roll has ruined their marriage. Rock and roll has ruined her life.

I am about to throw the Christmas card away when I notice the return address is in Phoenix. I study the little boy in the picture. He is flanked by well-groomed dogs and life-size nutcrackers, sitting in a wheelchair wrapped in tinsel. His limbs look like misprints. When I see he has my father's name I realize that this is my brother. He is nothing like how I pictured. I try to find traces of myself in his features but all I can see are his wheelchair and his sunglasses and his bedazzled T-shirt. ROCK LEGEND, it reads.

A year later. It is my first time in Tennessee. My dad and I are traveling 40 West to Memphis, Graceland-bound, like the song. We take trips like this every year because we both love America and American things like highways and country music and fast food. I open and close a little blue pillbox with Loretta Lynn's face on it. Five minutes earlier, I'd thrown it atop a pile of all things Loretta while checking out at Loretta Lynn's Country Store in Hurricane Mills, Tennessee.

"What do you need a pillbox for?" my dad said, laughing as if he didn't know: to keep my weed in. Duh.

Now we are listening to Loretta sing to Conway Twitty on a CD we just purchased also. My dad drums the rhythm on the steering wheel.

Love is where you find it
When you find no love at home
And there's nothin' cold as ashes
After the fire is gone

I wonder if this is why my dad cheats. He's looking for love elsewhere because he can't find the love at home. Sometimes I can't either. But I know it's there. Somewhere. I want to ask. But I find myself asking another question instead.

"Do you ever think about him?" I say finally.

"Who?" he replies.

"Your . . . my . . . your . . . your son."

He stops drumming. "You know, darling," he says, "I would. If he could think about me."

We are both quiet. Then he tells me the hotel in Memphis has ducks that ride in the elevator and pile into a fountain twice a day after walking down a red carpet. He does an impression of a duck in an elevator, using its bill to press the button. I laugh. The summer-blue sky is shining down on me. Loretta is still smiling up at me from the little pillbox.

I am twenty-two. My parents are getting that divorce. My dad has left my mom and is getting remarried. We aren't speaking. He lives in our old house with his new fiancée. One day I walk by and look in the window. On our fridge which had been painted like a blackboard they have written sweet nothings to each other in chalk. He has never been happier, his reads. From a photo online, I see his wardrobe reflects that. He has traded in the nice cashmere sweaters my mom bought him for crystals and love beads, his New Balances for leather sneakers. He has sideburns now.

I travel to shoot a movie on location in Hungary then gain thirty pounds. I joke it's because "I am very Hungary" but the real reason is I am very depressed and lonely. Fortunately, my mother comes to visit me. She is eating, praying, and loving herself around the world. I am so grateful to see her I weep. She has been to Rome to study cooking. Colorado to learn to whitewater raft. Now Budapest, to see me/cry while shopping for antiques. I am proud of her attempts at independence. We take a riverboat ride along the Danube and laugh because it is so cold and the food is bad. She shows me pictures on her phone: her frowning next to the Trevi Fountain. Her skulking in the Rockies. Her sitting next to my brother in Phoenix. Her and— I double back.

"Is that him?" I ask, shocked.

"I think it's time you two met."

In the cab from the airport, I think how the only other times I have been to Arizona were to visit my sisters in rehab. Now I am here to meet my father's son, who he had with another woman while he was still married to my mom. I wonder what the hell is wrong with Arizona. I decide it's the sun. There's too much of it. You cannot hide.

The house is at the end of a cul-de-sac. The other houses look empty. A large cactus rots out front. I ring the doorbell. A choir of dogs barks. A tall woman with stringy hair answers the door.

"Lilith?" I ask, a little surprised. From what I can tell of it, she is not my dad's type.

"I wish!" she says with a laugh before telling me she is Rhonda, the caretaker. Lilith, she says, is still on her daily run in the mountains. Lilith is very fit. She has the body of a teenager. Rhonda fends off the dogs, who are losing their minds. Clearly, they are not used to visitors, she says. This makes her laugh. But I just feel sad. Why does no one visit my brother? We walk past a dining room with its matching table and chairs. They look unused.

Rhonda tells me to have a seat on a very white couch in a very white living room, then disappears to finish getting my brother ready. A cinnamon-spice candle burns, almost covering up the faint smell of something bodily. A blow-dryer starts up. Rhonda sings over it. I notice a white plastic Christmas tree in a corner. And another in the kitchen. Both have lights on them. *Weird*, I think. It's July.

Above the television, there is a sign:

YOUR BAD PLANNING IS NOT MY EMERGENCY

I think how my mother would sooner die than hang a sign like that in our house, and I wonder whether my parents' marriage would have been easier if she had. A woman who decorates with Yankee candles and LIVE, LAUGH, LOVE–type signs seems simpler. A woman who prefers Diptyque and nude portraits of her children is more complicated. I notice a rig on the ceiling that snakes through the whole house. I feel like I'm in a very nice hospital. Maybe not so simple after all.

Rhonda is talking over the blow-dryer very loudly in the other room. "Are you ready to meet your big sis? She's soooo pretty! You are just gonna love her!"

I hear the blow-dryer shut off and brace myself.

My brother's shirt matches his bib. They are both a shocking blue. His legs are long and pale and he's wearing those same ski instructor–style sunglasses from the postcard. Rhonda parks his wheelchair across from me. I search for the right words and tone, but everything I can come up with sounds pat, like a badly written script. I would prefer to just hold him.

"Rhonda—what the hell!" Lilith says, bursting through the door. "I said no bib!"

She is sweating in all-black athleisure. She has dyed blond hair and a sparkly gel French manicure.

"Hi, Lola, it's so nice to meet you," she says, pitching her voice high, like she's doing a puppet show. She wipes a trail of spit from my brother's mouth. "I'm so embarrassed I had to do it with this silly little bib on!"

She takes his sunglasses off. His eyes go in different directions. They do not meet mine. Lilith shoots a look at Rhonda before offering me one of my brother's hands to shake. When I take it, it is soft and cold.

The sun is still out at my brother's bedtime. Lilith asks if I want to help. I say I do. She is matter-of-fact as she walks me through the routine. We remove an arc of stuffed animals from his bed methodically, as well as a few bedazzled pillows that say things like BOSS. I can't tell if she is being distant because she thinks of me as an enemy or because she is being respectful that I may see her as one. We lift my brother into bed. When he is tucked in, she leaves the room to give us time together. She says I can lie next to him if I want. I do.

"Hi," I say.

I imagine what he might say back.

After he falls asleep, I am surprised when Lilith asks if I want to go for dinner. I don't know what the right answer is. I am here because I want a relationship with my brother, not a relationship with a woman my father had a relationship with. But my brother cannot talk or walk or do much of anything on his own. To know him, I have to know her. Besides, I sort of like her. And I don't know anyone else in Phoenix.

She never goes out, she says, and gets very dressed up. I put on an old blue slip of my mom's I have stained. One of its spaghetti straps is held together with a safety pin. I have no bra on, and one of my boobs keeps threatening to fall out. I try to make up for this by applying more patchouli oil. When Lilith sees me, she looks at me like *You're wearing that?* and we both laugh. Our relationship begins and is very much founded on that exact sentiment. Our lives are so different, but there are things we share. A sense of humor about my choices. My little brother.

We go for margaritas and I drink several. It makes it easier to hear when she starts telling me what happened to my brother. There were complications with his birth. His umbilical cord was wrapped around his neck. The doctor used a vacuum to get him out quickly, so he wouldn't have brain damage. But she used it too much and his skull was too soft. The doctor damaged his brain. She said he'd be fine and for a while he was. But when he was two or so, he started knocking into things. It seemed like he couldn't see. Lilith took him to an eye doctor, who couldn't help. Then a neurologist, who did a brain scan.

"The part of the scan that's white is the part of his brain that is functioning," the neurologist said, pointing to the image. "The part that is gray is the part that isn't."

The scan was almost entirely gray. For the rest of my brother's life, the only thing he will be able to almost see are the kind of lights they put on Christmas trees.

A year later, I accidentally take too much acid at a party in L.A. the night before I'm supposed to fly back to Arizona. I keep hoping I won't be hallucinating by the time I have to board the flight, but no such luck. On the plane, I calm down enough to sleep a thick, hot sleep on the hour flight. When I wake up, the acid is making things shimmer instead of shake.

Rhonda and my brother greet me at baggage claim, as they usually do on my trips to Phoenix, which have become more frequent. I know this makes my mom feel bad because it means I see Lilith too. Even though things are civil between them, I try to minimize our relationship to my mother. I do not tell her that Lilith calls me her "favorite." I do not tell Lilith that this makes me uncomfortable because I suspect I am also my mom's favorite.

"There's your big sis!" Rhonda announces, waving like an inflatable figure outside a car dealership. When I am around my brother, I no longer have a name. I am just "big sis." It feels good. Even if I am not great at it. Even if sometimes I feel unworthy of it because I don't really know what I'm doing. After all, here is big sis on acid. I hold some crystals in place in his hands. I pretend I didn't just get them at the airport gift shop.

"Oooo, your big sis got you all these fun rocks!"

"Where to, Rhonda?" I ask, praying she'll say "bed" even though it's eleven a.m.

"The science museum!"

Oh boy! I think. *Oh. Fucking. Boy.*

A special telescope projects my eyeball across the width of the entire ceiling. I am amazed. My brother and I strap on helmets that measure brain activity. Whoever has the least brain activity shoots a little ball across a track the fastest. He wins. I put my arms through an astronaut costume. Rhonda poses my brother next to me. We take a photo.

"Houston, we have so many problems!" I joke.

This makes Rhonda laugh. I start to laugh too. Because I am so happy! Because I love my brother so much! I love how he smells and the sounds he makes! I love his long legs and the way his hair curls! I love how cute he looks when his mother dresses him like a five-year-old, even though I lecture her that she should dress him in cooler clothes because he's a teenager now! I love doing things for him! I love finding pieces of myself in his features! I think we have the same mouth! I love to imagine what he'd say if he could talk!

At his usual bedtime, four p.m., I crawl in with him. We sleep over fourteen hours. In the morning, we go to school.

My brother's school is nothing like the school I went to in Brooklyn, where African dance counted as gym and truancy was celebrated as a form of independence. It is very normal, like something out of a movie. Quarterbacks kiss cheerleaders against rows of lockers. Kids run when bells ring.

The special-ed classroom is located at the end of a long hallway. Today we are watching animal videos to prepare for an upcoming trip to the zoo.

Afterward, I push him around the track outside. A little girl grapevines over and sings a song from *Frozen* in my brother's face, then runs away.

"That's your brother's girlfriend," the teacher says.

"Really?" I reply. I look down at my brother. He doesn't seem particularly interested.

It's the championship game of the Little League season. My hands are around my brother's around the bat. A pitcher will throw the ball, and regardless of whether we hit it, I will get to push him around the bases. There are no losers. I am surprised to hear one of my dad's songs come on over the PA.

My dad has only met my brother twice. But Lilith acts

like he's never missed a game or bedtime. Like he doesn't act as if he doesn't have another son.

Back at the house, I watch Lilith dry my brother's hair before bed. She puts deodorant on him. All of his products are Axe. I think how he smells like boys I knew in middle school, preparing themselves to be men. She lays him out naked on a mat to put lotion on him. He makes a stretch noise. I notice some stubble around his groin.

"Do you shave him?" I ask, a little too surprised.

"Yup," she snaps. "It's a lot harder to clean him if I don't. Unless, of course, you wanna try?"

Lilith and my dad aren't the only ones acting as if. I am too. A real big sister would already know that.

His eighteenth birthday. Lilith has arranged for a neighbor to give him a ride in a Ferrari. They take photos of him in the driver's seat. I am hungover after a night in Vegas, eating a piece of his car-shaped cake with my hands. I say we should have hired some strippers. Lilith jokes I'm a bad influence, and I think how I probably would be, but my brother is incorruptible. She takes a picture of me and him wearing our matching do-rags I bought for us last-minute at a gas station because I forgot to get him a real present. I pose next to him making an ironic tough face. I still smell like alcohol from the night before. I look and feel like a caricature of a shitty father.

"Don't post that one," I say, because I am bloated. Also because she posts everything.

Sometimes I don't mind. I think this is the way it should be and should have been. Other times I do mind. Because it isn't this way. It never was. It is far more complicated. We are just pretending it isn't.

"She wanted him to leave us, you know!" my mom tells me each time I tell her I'm in Phoenix. "She's no saint!"

I consider my mom's very real pain, as I watch Lilith through the guest bedroom window. Lilith had a child with a married man. Now Lilith is lowering that child into the pool by herself with the assistance of a crane.

My sisters and I visit our brother together only once. Mino gives him Reiki. Emi pops a pimple on his back. We laugh a lot. We are different when we are trying to help someone else instead of trying to hurt each other. It feels like a strange dream of who we could have been. For a moment it is real.

"I just wish we'd known sooner," Emi says to me later that night. She is staring at the fan whirring on the popcorn ceiling. We are lying in the guest bed.

"I wish we'd known about him too," I say.

"No," she says, "I mean I wish we'd known how much more there was to life."

She turns on her side, away from me, and cries until she falls asleep. But I can't sleep because I can't stop thinking. I think how we grew up believing that a certain kind of beauty and level of success would win us love. I think how my mom probably only oriented us around those ideals so we might feel as she never did: desired. Secure. If we had beauty and success to offer in spades, our hearts might never stop momentarily with the shock of discovering secret children hidden in distant desert cities.

The next day we take a picture before we leave. My sisters and I surround our little brother. For a moment we are oriented around a different kind of beauty. Another kind of success.

There is cake at my brother's funeral because he died so close to his birthday. He was nineteen. My mother has sent flowers. Lilith displays them in the center of the house because, of all the ones she has received, my mother's are the most beautiful. Lilith releases a hundred white doves. My father makes a speech, which makes me angry. I wonder why Lilith lets him. But the fact is, my father is my brother's dad. In spite of everything, I am grateful he is mine too.

When it's all over and everyone has left, I go into my brother's room one last time. Above his bed there's a caricature of him from one of his birthday parties a while back, when Lilith hired a cartoonist. In the drawing, he stands upright, handsome and smiling, holding a pair of drumsticks in his hands. A little word bubble floats by his mouth. "Rock on!" he's saying.

THE STRAIGHT MAN

With the exception of all the times I have played gay, for the bulk of my career as an actress, I have been the straight man. As the uptight foil wrapped around the whimsy of another, cooler character, I couldn't help but feel miscast. Couldn't they see my glamour? Sense my daring? I was bold! Fun! *Not* the quiet assistant you threw dry cleaning onto. Wasn't it obvious I never stopped talking? Or was I too adept at playing the role I'd felt relegated to in my own family drama? The less-exciting-but-more-likely-to-remember-what-time-an-appointment-was one? The comparatively together one? The subordinate? The snooze?

It didn't help that Emi, who had never even wanted to act, gained success playing character after character who shared in her power, sex appeal, and aloofness. For so long, I had held out hope that a career as an actress would be my road to redemption. A way out of my sister's shadow. Instead, it just seemed to lead me right back into it.

Of course, I shouldn't have been too surprised. Alma, the family psychic, who for a brief period had lived with us in the room down the hall from mine, had predicted this years ago.

"She's gonna be a *HUGE* star," she said one night during a reading.

It was the summer between my freshman and sophomore years of college. My own career wouldn't begin for a while yet and Emi's was off to a rocketing start, after landing the breakout role in a hit TV show about sexy, floundering women in New York City.

"She was supposed to be the painter!" I wailed, hoping our familial roles might still count for something. "Not the actress!"

"Well, she's really good at it," Alma said apologetically.

"I know!" I sobbed. It was true.

"If it's any consolation, she'll never find happiness," Alma offered.

"Don't tell me psychic shit like that!" I replied, feeling as protective of Emi as I was enraged by her. Ah, sisterhood.

"Oh, that's not psychic," Alma replied. "That's just the sense I get from knowing her."

I felt for Emi a moment before redirecting the conversation back toward my favorite topic. "What about me?"

"I'll have to call in Archangel Michael."

From experience, I knew this was my cue to get very quiet and listen as she chanted like a Buddhist monk crossed with a sultry lounge singer. Her face started to move like a chipmunk chewing a small acorn.

"Oh, stop it!" she yelled at no one in particular, then to me, "Not *you*, the *guides*."

"I know," I said, impatient to uncover my destiny. This wasn't my first rodeo.

She snapped at the air again, then made a sound with her mouth like a CD skipping. "Weird . . . They're saying, 'It's not a food'?"

"I've been eating a lot of mushrooms lately?" I said, annoyed, as this seemed irrelevant to how I was going to become famous.

"Oh, right, that must be it," she said, her eyes closed. I rolled mine. "Okay, guides, she'll stop doing that"—she opened one eye to wink at me—"but we need to know when Lola will get her *big break*."

A moment later she was cocking her head far to the left. "That's odd," she said. "They're saying it's not going to be on TV."

"That's totally fine by me," I said gratefully. I knew I was meant for the big screen.

"But they're also saying it's *not film*."

"Well, what is it then?" I demanded. "Theater?" This would be fine. I would just need to rethink my imaginary penthouse. Or marry well.

"No," she said sadly, opening her eyes.

"*COMMERCIALS?*" I screamed.

"No!" she assured me, as if that were the lowest of the low. "*No. They're just saying that whatever your big break is doesn't exist yet.*"

Despondent, I made the short trip from her room to mine. Face down on my bed, I pictured myself selling futuristic Tupperware on QVC.

A few years later, at twenty-two, I was relieved when it seemed the psychic was wrong and I landed my first big acting job: the lead role in an indie movie. Directed by a giant of the form, the film followed a bookish college freshman who moves to New York, where she becomes transfixed by a manic-pixie-dream-girl-older-sister type. While I was appreciative, I couldn't help but think how perfect I could be in the role I wasn't playing. I'd lived in the city since I was four! I'd been smoking since I was fourteen! I was no ingenue. But it would be fine to sacrifice a bit of my real-life worldliness for the character's naivete. It would show my range. Besides, it was only a matter of time before everyone realized how sophisticated I truly was and I'd never have this problem again. Apparently, my character held similar beliefs.

"I could be the most beautiful woman in the world," I said, as her. "If only I could just get my look together."

Perhaps I was more suited to the role than I'd imagined.

After a few months of six-day weeks and seventeen-hour days, I was beginning to wonder if being an actress would ever make me feel beautiful at all. Filmmaking was far less glamorous than I'd imagined. The McDonald's bathroom in Times Square was as close as I got to a trailer. An active college dorm during an outbreak of influenza was our primary filming location. Even so, I loved it. I loved the script. The shared language of a film crew that no one else could understand. The characters, both on- and off-screen. It felt like we were a family. A large family rife with dysfunction. Which is to say: *my* family, and that was sort of the problem.

I found myself feeling as confused about my place and worth on set as I had at home: in the way, even though I was assured that I belonged. Important yet not. Was I doomed to re-create this dynamic over and over and throughout eternity? Or was I just seeking out the spaces in which it already existed, to feel comfortable, because that discomfort was all I'd ever known?

After a particularly brutal day on set, when my beautiful, cool costar hadn't said anything after the director said my skin was so bad it looked like I'd "put a pizza" on my face, in front of the whole crew, I sought refuge with my family.

"I thought you loved her, though," Emi replied blankly.

I had forgotten how I'd used my relationship with the actress to try to make my sister jealous. Shit.

"I do!" I backpedaled. "I just wish she would have told him I'm breaking out because the cinematographer doesn't wash his brushes after he applies my concealer!"

"Why is the cinematographer applying your concealer?" she asked, appropriately puzzled. Normally, cinematographers are just concerned with cameras.

"Because he doubles as the makeup artist!"

"Weird," she said. "I get my own personal makeup artist."

I felt worse than I had before our conversation. My big little indie movie had nothing on her hit TV show. Of course she had her own makeup artist. Of course she did.

One afternoon, after I'd eaten fifty mozzarella sticks because we'd done as many takes of a scene in which my character eats just one, my agent called. With the tone of a game show host in a toupee, he told me how a website that typically sold books was now making TV shows. Except the TV shows would be played not on an actual TV but on your computer. The whole thing sounded dubious until I remembered Alma's words: *Whatever your big break is doesn't exist yet.*

When he mentioned that a foreign film star I'd spent my adolescence getting off to was attached to star, my imagination went wild. Perhaps this was the vehicle that would thrust me out of my sisterly shadow and into the warm glow of Hollywood's spotlight! Not to mention a passionate lifelong love affair with my childhood crush! I began preparing for the audition right away. I got the part.

A few months later, filming began on location in New York City. Instantly, it was clear this was going to be much closer to what I'd always thought starring in something would be like. There were actual makeup artists. I had a real trailer instead of the handicapped stall in McDonald's. There was a whole table *with every snack imaginable and:* there were people who went to that table *whenever I asked them to and brought me things.*

"Could I have the trail mix mixed in with extra M&M's?" I'd ask. It took a lot for me not to order them to pick out the green ones.

"Could I have those peanut-butter pretzels from Costco but *mixed* with the chocolate-covered raisins also from Costco?"

The life I'd always dreamed of was unfolding. I was allowed to eat whatever I wanted, *and* people were always happy to see me. Well, most people. Except the foreign film star, who we'll just call FFS for short. But I didn't take it personally. He was going through a breakup. I was patient. With time, I knew he'd be happily married. To me.

"I feel sad," he confided to me one afternoon a few weeks

in. Things were looking up: we were sitting in our cast chairs while he touched my weenus. Evidently, it gave him comfort to fondle the loose skin on my elbow because he thought it was very soft.

"I can only imagine," I said, edging my elbow a little closer, like a mother pushing a blanket on a sad child.

It wasn't just romance I was gunning for. Watching him act was an education. I marveled at the way he improvised and mined the humor in everything he did. I wanted to be like that too. While I envied his ability to take up space, I knew it would be out of place for my demure character to do the same. The show would be better served by my remaining straight-faced whenever his character said something insane. The smaller I was, the bigger he could be. It was sort of like the way I'd felt growing up with my family, except now it served a purpose: it made the show better.

Fortunately, off-screen I was beginning to feel more like his equal. He made me laugh and I made him laugh too. As he didn't live in New York and I did, I tried to find things for him to do and for us to do together to make him feel more at home/fall in love with me.

During one night shoot, we were sitting in his trailer between scenes. He was homesick and he needed a friend, and since I was that, there we were.

"Would you like to be my date to a fancy dinner?" he asked.

"Um." I hesitated. "I feel like maybe I shouldn't, 'cause I'm sorta seeing someone now?"

It was true. I had recently started a whirlwind romance with a long-haired musician type named Ian. FFS smiled understandingly. Still, I felt a little like I'd let him down. Like a big brother, he often spoke of wanting big things for me. There was one very specific fantasy I didn't quite understand, in which I lived alone in Sri Lanka with a small cat. And another in which I worked with Jake Gyllenhaal because FFS thought I looked like him. I knew a boyfriend would make such things more difficult. But I liked my boyfriend.

The next day, Mino called to tell me that FFS had asked her on a date.

I was stunned. I had introduced them a few weeks earlier at my niece's birthday, but I hadn't been aware they'd exchanged numbers.

"Wait, aren't you seeing someone?" I asked.

"We broke up!"

"When?"

"This morning."

"You don't happen to be going with him to a fancy dinner, do you?" I asked dubiously.

"Yes!" she squealed.

As soon as we hung up, FFS entered the makeup trailer.

After greeting each person with a long hug that evolved into a sort of salsa step, he sat down in the chair next to me. When I ignored him, he gave my shoulder a friendly shake.

"So, my sister, eh?" I said with the warmth of a woman scorned.

"Yes!" He gleamed, cheerful. "She is so nice!"

The day carried on without an issue. I began to wonder if maybe there was nothing weird about him asking me out, then dating my sister. It wasn't like it hadn't happened before.

That night, Mino texted me: His eyes are AMAZING and he's so funny we had the best time!!!

The message made me happier than I'd expected. Maybe FFS and I were really better suited as friends. If all went well, I thought, we might even be relatives. I was warming up to the thought when I received a text from him: Your eyes are big as suns. You are the best!

Work went as usual the next day. We were filming on location in Queens. Except when I returned to my trailer after lunch, I found Mino inside.

"What are you doing here?" I gasped.

"Oh, I was just in the neighborhood!"

"You were just *in Flushing*?" Sure, we'd been raised in New York. But not *this* New York.

"Yeah!" she chirped. "So . . . where is he?"

A moment later, there was a knock on my trailer door. It was him.

"Lola!" he said, sounding surprised to see me. "What are you doing here?"

"This is my trailer," I declared.

He beelined toward my sister.

Before bed that night, Mino wrote again: He's coming over Saturday!

A moment later, FFS texted: You make me so happy!

I spent the weekend in a confused rage. Who was this psycho seeing my sister and simultaneously confessing feelings for me? When Monday rolled around, I didn't speak to him unless scripted.

"What's wrong with you?" he mouthed between takes.

I averted my gaze.

At lunch, I sat alone and stared at the wall in my trailer, which shared a wall with his. I heard him laughing on the phone with someone I assumed was Mino. When silence returned, I got up and knocked on his trailer door.

"Lola!" He had the look of a concerned teacher. "Please come in!"

"Look," I said, beginning a speech I'd prepared. "You can't *date my sister* AND send me texts every night telling me my eyes are 'big as suns'!"

He looked perplexed. "But why?" he said innocently. "They *are* big as suns!"

I caught a glimpse of them in the mirror. They were rather large. How had I never noticed that before?

"Okay, well, then you can't date my sister *and* message me saying you think I'm the best!"

"But I do!" he replied emphatically. *"Because you are my friend!"*

"So you just tell all your friends stuff like that?" I asked, incredulous.

"Sometimes, yes. But not everyone has eyes big as suns. So unless they do, I do not tell that to them."

As we made up, I couldn't help but feel struck by how similar our misunderstanding had been to those our characters would often have. Interactions like these were the spine of our show's humor: his larger-than-life character would lob outrageous desires in my quiet one's direction. Then she'd have to figure out a way to accommodate or squash his whims entirely. In essence, he'd act out and she'd clean up, the very way I felt I'd been doing with my family for my whole life. I was typecast, as I'd feared, not miscast, as I'd hoped.

But art only imitates life with an eye toward expanding it. It changes our minds by opening them, letting light in where there wasn't any. With a little illumination, I was able to see the great arcs I'd long failed to notice. Eventually, "the straight man" always curves in order to travel his own crooked path. He is not just a narrative device for another character's growth. He transforms too, often leaving the viewer to wonder: who is the foil for whom?

PART THREE

Sex Work, Merkins, and Country Music

Well-behaved women seldom make history.

—A bumper sticker I hate

HEAVEN

My relationship with Ian began a few months into shooting with FFS, at five a.m. on my twenty-fourth birthday, in a rented RV, at a music festival. It continued as a cyclone of sex, drugs, and road trips, then almost ended a year later, when we were apprehended by Amtrak police aboard a train headed west. Tipped off by accounts of "suspicious behavior," the cops burst into our sleeper car to discover me playfully bound by a pair of white stockings and wearing little else. Fortunately, they found nothing to warrant our arrest—the poor suckers couldn't find our stash—and the incident only made us stronger. Ian decided to quit drinking and drugs, and I was happy for him, even if I was a little unhappy for me. He'd also resolved, it seemed, to quit sex.

But things were good enough. Within a few months, we left the temptations of New York City behind us and moved across the country. Though I had never thought much of Los Angeles, Ian considered the word "Californian" to be a high compliment he was hell-bent on one day receiving. With the success of my TV show and the other films I had done so far, the relocation actually made sense. We rented a little red house on a small hill. I tried to adjust to the suburban quiet of L.A. life.

One afternoon, in our backyard dotted with jasmine and bird-of-paradise, a friend named Elsie asked if I'd take her photo.

"I mean, sure, but I'm not very good," I warned her.

"Oh, it doesn't matter. It just can't be a selfie."

She brought over a bunch of shapeless white garments to wear, then stood against random trees in my yard, shifting easily between smiling and pouting.

"What's this for?" I asked.

"My new job. It's a massage thing."

A few weeks later, she invited me to dinner. *She must be broke*, I thought, since I was used to paying for her. When the check came, Elsie reached for it.

"Thanks!" I said a little too loudly, betraying my surprise.

"Of course, Lo." She smiled graciously. "I'm doing really well at the moment."

She looked it too. Elsie was glowing. I wondered if she was doing more yoga than usual or if she'd switched her meds.

"I work at a dojo, you know."

"Oh! Cool," I said, too embarrassed to admit I didn't know what a dojo was.

"It's called Heaven."

"Is this the massage thing you mentioned?"

"Yes!" She smiled.

I wasn't surprised. Elsie was very tactile. I enjoyed spending time with her for many reasons, not least of which was she'd spontaneously rub my shoulders, hands, and feet. I am a glutton for touch.

"It's really special." Her eyes glazed over with melancholic joy. The work was penetrating some deeply neglected part of her soul. "I mean, sometimes I just feel like I'm giving old men hand jobs—"

"*What?*"

"But for the most part I feel like I'm healing people, and they are symbiotically healing me."

"Wait." I studied Elsie's face for a long time, expecting to find some visible mark of the change she was suggesting. Fangs, maybe. Or a gold tooth. Instead, she just radiated. Still, I had to ask. "Are you a hooker?" I whispered.

"It's a form of sex work, yes," she answered.

"I'm so sorry," I said, immediately aware that I'd made a classist, anti-feminist faux pas.

When I got home that night, Ian was already in bed. He'd recently become absorbed in the collected works of a South African novelist and wasn't leaving the house much because he was trying to stay sober. While I knew this was all probably for the best, it was a bit boring. I hoped my news might shake things up a little.

"Ian!" I gasped. "Elsie is . . . *a sex worker!*"

"Huh?" He spooned the last of a sugar-free pint of ice cream into his mouth—he wasn't doing that either. Or gluten. He was still smoking, though. Thank God.

"You know, like a *prostitute*! Though we're not supposed to say that anymore."

"Weird."

He seemed nonplussed. I resented his capacity to mind his own business. Ian was attuned to the finer things in life, which made him impossible to go on walks with. They took forever. He was always stopping to photograph a flower or beam at a pair of rainbows.

"She jerks off old dudes at this place called Heaven!"

With this, he put his book down, I opened my laptop, and we googled it.

Heaven had locations in New York, San Francisco, and both the Eastside and Westside of Los Angeles. We scoured the website, browsing through the profiles of the women. One of them was a friend's girlfriend we'd just been camping with. Another was a girl who'd been in my poetry class at college. We were stunned.

"This one enjoys deep breathing and is a Level Three dojo master," I said, still wondering what a dojo was as I took in the selection. When I realized most of the women looked like Ian's ex-girlfriends, I grew concerned. Feeling sexually rejected by him was beginning to make me doubt myself. I worried maybe I wasn't very good in bed, which wouldn't have surprised me. I am the same with sex as I am with dancing: largely unskilled but enthusiastic should a song I like be playing.

"Are you attracted to them?" I asked as we scrolled past beautiful woman after woman. There was Dream Wilder, who was passionate about herbalism, full release, and the present moment. Allegra Arcosanti, who was just there "to serve you." Jöy Sol, who had a misplaced umlaut.

"I mean, sure, some of them are beautiful."

"What if this were my job?"

"You don't need a job. You're on a TV show."

"A *streaming* show," I corrected. "And no, I know, but if I needed money, this would probably be better than like being a barista."

He looked at me like I was a spoiled brat, then reminded me how I hated giving hand jobs, which would make working at a place like Heaven impossible. But maybe if we looked at the website long enough, we could get inspired and *pretend* like I did . . . or not. A few minutes later, Ian was fast asleep. I lay awake for hours, feeling deprived, as usual. Another night when we didn't have sex. Another night when I felt old and ugly when I could be feeling young and beautiful.

Throughout my childhood, my mother had insisted that I act "age-appropriately." Then her demand had only confused me, as it conflicted with her persistent need for me to sort through decidedly age-inappropriate issues. Suddenly I wondered: should I have been able to see past her actions and taken her words more seriously? Having been a wife and mother since she was nineteen, my mom had spent her own youth burdened with responsibility for others. I could see now that she was likely trying to protect me from doing the same. But I had been dead set on finding the love I couldn't at home. At twenty-seven, I'd had a rotating cast of serious boyfriends since I was twelve. I had barely been single. Now I just wanted to be free and unencumbered. Like neither I nor my mother had ever been. Like Elsie.

A few weeks later, Elsie invited me to an art show downtown that featured two redheads drawing over each other's naked bodies while screaming. The gallery was hot and smelly. I whispered jokes into Elsie's ear to lighten the mood. She smiled serenely at me. When the piece ended and I realized they weren't serving wine, I left. Back at my car in the desolate L.A. parking lot, I was surprised to discover a beautiful woman in a large, fluffy hat standing next to it.

"Think I could get a ride?" she asked. She had a large cold sore on her lip, almost completely covered by a heart-shaped jewel.

"Where are you going?" I asked, remembering my desire to retrieve my youth and freedom, thinking this was what youthful, free people did. That or what people about to be strangled to death did. Either way—you miss a hundred percent of the shots you don't take.

"East," she cooed.

"Hop in," I relented.

Her name was Hart, which sounded fake but what do I know. Mine is Lola Clementine. Hart was one of those people who didn't mind quiet. As I do, I interrogated her.

"So what's your job?" I asked, reminding myself of my grandfather, a serious, cigar-smoking man whose Wikipedia page describes him simply as having been "a tycoon."

"Oh." She laughed. "Well, I'm an actress."

After living in L.A., the word had come to possess the same power that the word "finance" once had: immediately, I'd stop paying attention. But her professions didn't stop there.

"And I'm a musician. And a chef. And an artist. And I do spoken-word— Oh, it's this street," she said, pointing to mine.

"Oh my God!" I yelled. "Neighbors!"

Suddenly, it clicked: a few days earlier, Ian had come back from a neighborhood walk to report that he had seen a woman, completely naked, doing gymnastics in her front yard.

"Did you see her vagina?" I scoffed.

"What do you think?" he replied. "She was naked in happy baby!"

At the time I'd felt jealous. I wanted to be the only woman he saw naked. I also wanted to be the kind of woman who felt free enough to just be naked. Maybe not in happy baby but in downward dog, or something like it. I had wondered who this intrepid being was. Now I knew: she was in my front seat.

"Thank you for the ride, baby angel queen!" she said, gathering her faux furs to leave. A drum circle, it seemed, was starting up in her backyard.

"Hey—I really like to dance," I found myself saying, thinking this was the type of activity she would gravitate toward. I hoped some of her ample freedom would rub off on me by osmosis.

"I love to dance!" she agreed.

"Great! Well, sometimes I dance naked in my garden," I lied.

Her expression remained kindly blank.

"So if you ever wanna join me, just come over. It's a great workout."

"Ugh! I love working out!" She was ecstatic.

"Really? I hate it."

"Oh well, I have to." Hart smiled. "I do porn." She kissed me on the mouth before skipping up her steps.

At home, Ian was deep into the seventh season of *The West Wing*.

"I met the girl whose vagina you saw!" I announced as I walked in.

"That's amazing, babe!" He was eating a bag of gluten-free cookies, probably laughing at something charming Josh had said. He turned the bag inside out to hunt for scraps as I began to undress slowly in the doorway. His eyes remained glued to the screen. I moved to turn off the TV.

"What are you doing?" Ian asked.

"Do you want to see . . . *my vagina?*"

There was a pause.

"Well, I'm looking at it right now," he said with a laugh.

I stormed into the other room and threw myself face down onto the couch.

"Why can't you be sexy?" I wailed.

"Are you getting your period?"

"I had it last week!" I sobbed.

He said nothing.

"You make me feel old! I wanna be wild! I wanna be free!" I continued.

He chuckled like a loving parent.

"How can you just stand there and laugh at me?" I demanded.

"Because you already are free, Lola."

He walked into the guest bedroom and shut the door quietly behind him.

I spent more and more time with Hart over the following weeks. She was friends with Elsie too and occasionally picked up shifts at Heaven. For someone so free, she was oddly reliable. I didn't care that I didn't understand what she was saying half the time or felt embarrassed when I noticed contradictions in her stories. I liked her stand on capitalism and how she always smelled like vetiver mixed with cigarettes mixed with tanning oil. I even introduced her to my mother when she came into town. After, Hart wept as she held me close.

"I've never met anybody so mean in my life," she said, sobbing.

"Really?" I said, surprised. "I thought she was pretty nice to you!"

"To you, Lo. To *you*!"

A few weeks later, the poppies were in bloom and all of East L.A. lost their minds. Fleets of Subarus lined rural roads. Young people took pictures of their friends to post to Instagram, captioned with lyrics from '60s songs about revolution. Ian wanted to make the trip to the premier poppy-viewing spot. But by then I just wanted to break up, and took the hour-long drive as an opportunity to do so. When we finally arrived, Ian refused to venture in. He didn't want to contaminate the natural phenomenon with our toxicity. Instead, we sat on the hood of the car, trying to sort out our lives.

"Is this really what you want, Lola?"

"I don't know!" I replied, wondering if Ian was right. Maybe I wasn't starved for freedom. Maybe I was smothered by it. I considered taking it all back and telling him how much I loved him. Instead, I heard myself asking if he wanted to get a couples massage at Heaven.

He wasn't interested but said I was free to if I wanted. He owed me a birthday present, anyway. I went online to peruse my options. It would be weird to select our friend's girlfriend or the girl from Intro to American Poetry. Parvati Pelligrino was older and would have appealed to me if she hadn't had so much Botox. Aurelia Steele looked a little scary. Eventually, I landed on Indigo Blue. While her pseudonym was by far the most redundant, she looked sort of like someone I could feasibly pick up at a bar, so I went for it.

I sent my inquiry through their website, then texted with Elsie and Hart to notify them of my upcoming adventure. They were excited and encouraged me to share my experience of "the work" with them after, a sentiment they each punctuated with various nature-themed emojis.

For fear of running into other clients, I decided not to go to the dojo* itself and booked a hotel. Plus, I reasoned, if it were fun, perhaps Ian could join us after. But on the day in question, Ian had the flu. I made him some soup to compensate for the fact that he was paying for me to fuck someone else. Then I slipped into a red lace lingerie set. I was unsure whether or not I was supposed to seduce Indigo Blue back, but I wanted to at least be prepared. It felt rude to assume the experience would be so transactional, even though that was the whole point.

In the lobby on a red velvet sofa, I changed the cross of my legs about eighteen times. It was a quiet afternoon, and

---

* "A room or hall in which judo and other martial arts are practiced." —*Oxford English Language Dictionary*

the hotel was far less fancy in reality than it had been in my mind. I feared everyone knew exactly what I was there for. I picked up a newspaper and tried to read it. Bad things were happening. My libido was dwindling. I put the paper down and stared at my shoes.

"Anna?" someone called.

"Anna?" I heard again before remembering that Anna was my alias.

"Indigo?" I asked, hoping I was wrong. She looked a lot younger than she had in her picture.

"Hi!"

When I stood up to greet her, I hulked over her. She was tiny. I smelled her breath when she smiled. It was bad. My stomach sank. Could I ask her to brush her teeth? Or was that rude? What would a man do?

In the elevator, I remembered how ineffective I'd always been at seducing women. The truth was: they scared the shit out of me. Any brief burst of queerness I'd experienced earlier in my twenties had relied heavily on the other's prowess. Left to my own devices, I'd sully all potential lesbian encounters with too much information about my childhood and too many questions about their mothers. As the elevator ascended, Indigo Blue and I smiled awkwardly at each other. Then I reminded myself that she was being paid to touch my vagina. I made a bad joke to calm my nerves. When she laughed, I smelled her breath again. I was considering faking a family emergency when the doors opened on our floor. It was too late.

Once in the room, I announced I was going to shower, hoping she might join and there might be a toothbrush and some overpriced French toothpaste on hand. No such luck. When I reemerged, she was setting up an altar of colored rocks by the window. She invited me to sit down on the bed. I did, but I couldn't stop thinking about how to politely ask her to brush her teeth. The capitalist in me reasoned that since money was being exchanged, I could make any demand I wanted. But the woman in me won out. I would say nothing and forgo breathing altogether.

I stripped down to my underwear quickly and sat on the bed to watch her undress, which seemed to take hours. Her outfit had so many layers. She looked like a beloved teapot in a cozy. Finally, she was naked, except for some natural deodorant (didn't work) and a large, badly drawn tattoo of a feather. She sat down across from me and exhaled. I wilted like a cartoon bouquet.

She gazed into my eyes, which scared me a little.

"You're so beautiful," I said, just to say something.

Her smile widened. I breathed through my mouth.

"Thank you," she said, blushing. "So are you."

As she began to chant, I considered her body in comparison to mine. Her stomach was flat. Mine wasn't. Did she think it was ugly? Did she find me attractive? Did she feel I was free for doing something like this? Did I feel she was free, at five hundred dollars for two hours?

Her small breasts bounced gently as she adjusted herself. She placed her whole palm over my underwear and began to move it in a circular motion. Her chanting intensified. Since I wasn't aroused, I began to fantasize about a porn I saw once.

"May I enter you?" she asked tenderly.

"Um . . ."

"It's just an option." She smiled.

"I'm okay, thank you."

She kept on with the circular motion as I stared at her tits. I was grateful when I came.

As we dressed after, I tried to make conversation.

"So do you have other jobs?"

"Oh sure," she replied. "I'm an actress, and a musician, and a writer. All kinds of things."

"That's cool," I said. "Me too, I guess."

Finally, she was clothed. When she didn't exit swiftly, I realized she was waiting for me to tip her.

"Oh!" I panicked. "I'm sorry, I don't have any cash. Can I do it through the website later?"

"That won't work," she said with a frown.

"Do you do Venmo?"

She had to give me her number so I could find her on the app. It was connected to her real name, which I didn't want to look at out of respect, but I couldn't help it. It was so ordinary; Indigo Blue suited her better. I tipped her a hundred bucks.

"Good luck with everything!!!" I wrote in the comments.

THE COWBOY PROBLEM

I felt guilty accepting the invitation.

For one, Ian and I still weren't in a great place. For two, it was to a songwriting retreat. Sure, I'd been playing and writing music on my own and with friends since I was a teenager. But over the four years we'd been together, our musical lives had grown very much entwined. After all, it was Ian who'd tolerated my out-of-tune guitar and off-key singing. Ian with whom I played for tips and no one, up and down the West Coast, before dashing off alone to fancy film sets. Ian always wanted the best for me, even when I easily got the kinds of things he'd worked so hard for, like an all-expenses-paid trip to a songwriting retreat. Sheepishly, I assured him the experience would be a good networking opportunity. Generously, he assured me I deserved things like this. After a roadhouse gig together in Montana, he drove home to L.A. while I flew to a strange billionaire's home on Nantucket.

201

It was early September, and the village had that end-of-season emptiness that made me melancholy as a child but felt sort of romantic as an adult. Two emissaries of the retreat picked me up at the dock—Jerry, a large man with wide eyes frozen in a state of uncertain dismay, and Gemma, a tiny woman with a voice like husky helium. A magnum of red wine was jammed in the cupholder between them.

"That's the post office," Gemma chirped as we drove through town.

"That's my house," Jerry said, nonchalant.

"But *we* don't live there." Gemma chuckled, sticking her hand between Jerry's giant thighs.

"Why not?" I asked.

Gemma giggled suggestively.

"Because his wife does."

Jerry took a long slug of wine. Gemma hit him playfully. Island shit.

"Jerry! You're driving!"

When we arrived at the property, Jerry showed me around. The house was large but quaint and belonged to a billionaire whose family had made its fortune slinging baby products. With a passion for Prince and expensive guitars, the billionaire had Jerry outfit the old barn as a recording studio. Since the billionaire was busy and rarely used said studio, he decided to open it up to others, to the benefit of his taxes and the lives of many musicians. A few hours later, I met my songwriting fellows. There were five men who were perfectly nice and two women, Ella and Crystal, with whom

I became fast friends due to a shared love of drinking, singing, and complaining.

A week in, things were going swimmingly when Ella dropped the exciting news that a "hot guy" was coming. The three of us squealed—but quietly. We all had long-term boyfriends back home.

"He's a really successful music producer," Ella continued, "*and* . . . he's a *cowboy*."

I had first been turned on to cowboys in college, when Ada showed me the *Pat Garrett and Billy the Kid* soundtrack. Thoughts of the Wild West had consumed me. It was nice to imagine somewhere more lawless than the lawlessness I'd known in the West Village. I liked escaping into a land of cowboys, who were all-American and ruggedly independent, unlike me, who was tenuously British and fiercely codependent.

In preparation to finally meet one, I would need some new clothes—after all, the weather was changing. And maybe a new skin-care regime, as my skin was beginning to show signs that I'd consumed nothing but cheese, whiskey, and wine for days. And, of course, we'd have to prepare a home-cooked feast. To welcome him with. I went into the village and spent a small fortune. When I returned, I had a frozen chicken under one arm, an array of chunky knits in the other, and a face dotted in zit cream. I hoped to be acne-free for the Cowboy that evening. But when I stepped into the kitchen, I found him already there. Sitting at the kitchen table, wearing Wrangler everything, he looked like he'd recently dismounted a horse.

"Hello," he said, his voice deep and Texan. He spun a wineglass sophisticatedly between his fingers. Instantly, I knew I wanted to be with him forever. And not just because his jeans were so tight, I could basically see his dick.

Over the next week, we three women followed him like thirsty cattle. The Cowboy was like a wild spring of secure masculinity that had seemingly run dry in California. He was silly. He was smart. He paid for things. He was fun. Never mind that he owned guns and wore much too much cologne. He was in therapy! Only the Texan kind—which diverged slightly from the Freudian sort I'd been in since I was ten, as it entailed copious amounts of Coors Light and '80s country on a jukebox.

Night after night, the four of us would stay up talking after everyone else had gone to sleep. When one of us women would inevitably start to cry, he was nothing but understanding: life was full of disappointments. The music business was hard. Men were awful. At least the ones who weren't him. He was perfect.

As the threat of departure became increasingly real, Ella, Crystal, and I began doing very bizarre things to corral the Cowboy's attention. One evening, Ella took a drunken bath in his cottage's tub, fully clothed. On another, Crystal made us film her doing a dance in his bedroom while she wore an empty beer box on her head and sang in an eerie, high-pitched voice. Fortunately, their antics outweighed mine.

All I did was ask him to go skinny-dipping with me in a neighboring billionaire's pool. There, I made up a game that involved me chasing him underwater, naked.

"If I were a woman," he said to me as we dried ourselves off after, "I'd want to be you."

"Me too," I said. "But you."

It was true. The Cowboy embodied both the freedom and stability I'd long craved. He was like a wild horse in a round pen—easily able to follow life's demands without giving up who he really was. I had spent my whole life trying to strike that same balance, teetering between my family's confusing rules and the ones I was trying to write for myself, often only to crash-land on the ground below. Maybe it wasn't love I was falling into but aspiration I was feeling. Maybe it was both.

On our final night together, Ella, Crystal, and I dismantled his bed so we could reconstruct it on the grass outside under the stars. Summer was over. My heart was heavy. I didn't want to leave him. But I didn't want to lie next to him either, in case I liked it too much. As the four of us lay beneath the open sky, the other women began a last-ditch effort to crack his cowboy code.

"How many women have you slept with?" Ella pushed him.

"A gentleman doesn't kiss and tell," he replied, as if playing in a bad Western. Clearly he was tired of us.

"Do you wanna have babies?" Crystal asked.

He laughed. "I don't know!"

"Come on!" Ella taunted.

"I'll have your babies," I offered quietly.

The Cowboy's eyes caught mine. We stayed that way for a moment, until Crystal began to cry. The mushrooms were kicking in. The stars were just so beautiful.

On the ferry back to the mainland the next day, I was hungover and heartbroken. When I got home to L.A. that night, I was unusually monosyllabic.

"How was it?" Ian asked.

"Good."

"Did you make friends?"

"Yes."

"You didn't call that much?" Ian added.

"There just wasn't any goddamn service—JESUS, CAN WE NOT?"

The weeks that followed weren't any better. The quiet doubt I'd felt for years with Ian was now screaming at a fever pitch. I missed the Cowboy like crazy. But was it the Cowboy I was longing for? Or was it the tender balance I felt he embodied? There was only one way to find out: travel to Texas and make a country-duets record together. But I would be sensible. I would not fall in love with the Cowboy. Of course I would not fall in love with the Cowboy. I already was in love with the Cowboy.

At first, it was all very professional. We'd record in his studio during the day, then go our separate ways. A few nights in things shifted when I found myself saying the words "Honky Tonkin'" plus "take me." After all, I had a lot on my mind. I could benefit from some Texan therapy too.

A pickup truck that was an Uber took us to our first bar, where the only other patrons were a Mexican man and his Texan wife, there to celebrate his birthday. For the occasion, the woman had made a cake resembling the Rio Grande. Using blue-green icing for the river, she'd fashioned her husband out of marzipan, bursting through a row of upright graham crackers representing Trump's border wall. We ate some, then did karaoke. The Cowboy sang "Waltz Across Texas."

When we dance together, my world's in disguise
It's a fairyland tale that's come true
And when you look at me with those stars in your eyes
I could waltz across Texas with you

When he finished, I had to excuse myself to the bathroom so I could remove my underwear. I had gotten too wet to leave them on. Stuffing them in the pocket of my buckskin jacket, I reemerged to sing Patsy Cline's "Crazy," which was fitting, because that was what I was. Crazy. And commando.

When I finished, we took another Uber to another bar, which was even emptier. Just us and a busboy, who was watching a telenovela on his phone. The bartender, a buxom German, gave us a free round of shots.

"For ze beautiful couple!" she said, saluting.

I didn't correct her. After, I proposed. The Cowboy said yes, if we could find a place where I could also be married to Ian.

"Why?" I yelled.

"Because I know you love him too," the Cowboy replied. I supposed I did.

From there, we walked to a set-up bar, where the Cowboy and I were the only inhabitants under sixty. While I was trading earrings with a Svedka-drinking widow named Sharon, the Cowboy was catching up with the owner, a cigar-smoking man of about four hundred pounds named Lonnie. When we made our way back to each other, I asked him if he wanted to kiss me.

"I do," he replied.

His lips, which appeared wide and thin, felt endless on mine, like a magical room you might read about in a story-book, in which you discover a door to another world, or Texas itself, because there's just so much space. I felt myself expanding to fit them, old ideas contracting as I did. For so long, I'd believed I had to be wild to be free. Competitively reckless, I was perpetually guilty: creating more chaos didn't suit me. It conflicted too much with the role I'd assumed as a child: the one who'd believed she had to hold it all together as others tore it apart. But chaos was all I'd known. Wild actions, I believed, would liberate me, even if they hadn't yet, after I'd taken so many. Now here I was once again, acting wild. But as we two-stepped in the dark, I didn't feel wild anymore. Instead, I felt tame. But not entirely. Just like a domesticated wolf you could actually live with. I liked it.

In the morning, I took myself to the Cowgirl Hall of Fame, a popular local attraction. My duct-taped cowboy boots echoed in the wide Texan halls as I studied the women on the walls: Annie Oakley. Bridget "Biddy" Mason. Their wildness was different from the kind I'd grown up knowing in New York City. It had purpose. I felt inspired as I hopped in a photo booth that made it look as if I were parading across the Great Plains alongside these heroines. So inspired, in fact, that I flashed my boobs at the camera.

It was something I'd seen Emi do over a dozen times. The consummate youngest, I'd been copying my big sisters my whole life. Stealing their clothes and manners. Likes and dislikes. It wasn't just because I thought they were prettier. More interesting. It was also a matter of survival. The more like them I was, the less likely I felt they were to eat me. After all, they were wolves. Not cannibals. Taking my tits out in photos seemed like a great way to prove I was equally as wild. And, also, that I had a great rack. The picture would make the perfect keepsake for the Cowboy.

When I gave it to him that afternoon, he looked more

embarrassed than excited. Suddenly, I was too, as if it wasn't just my breasts I was baring, but the entirety of my existential confusion. In the face of his Texan modesty, my New York grandiosity shrank enough for me to perceive another possibility. Maybe I didn't need to be like my sisters to be valuable. Maybe I just needed to be me. Whoever that was. Whoever I'd found back there, in his arms, on the barroom floor. Only I'd have to be that me without him. After all, I still had a boyfriend.

Later, I tried to return a shirt the Cowboy had left in my hotel room one night.

"You can keep it," he said.

"No," I replied. His name had been printed inside by the dry cleaner. I couldn't take that home.

He looked away. I was beginning to reassure myself that what happens in Texas *maybe* could possibly remain in Texas when he started up again. "I'm moving to L.A. next week."

"What? Why?" It was the best and worst news I'd ever heard.

"I can't be here anymore."

I chugged my beer.

"Maybe we could have dinner sometime?"

"Maybe," I said.

The next morning, as I drove myself to the airport, I felt as lost as I truly was on the ten-lane Texas highway. Was it real that I could be the woman I'd found with the Cowboy instead of the other one I'd been practicing for so long? Or was that some story I was telling myself? A profound and lazy way of dismissing everything else in my life as a mistake instead of admitting I was making one? My shame was finally setting in. Mistake it was. I would never tell a soul.

A week later, the Cowboy texted to tell me he'd relocated to Los Angeles. Before replying, I called a friend, breaking my promise to myself and confessing what had happened.

Calmly, she explained that I was in "withdrawal."

"You're like an addict. He's your drug."

I winced. She sounded so stupid yet somehow so right. My phone dinged. It was the Cowboy again, asking if he could take me to dinner. Instead of responding, I downloaded a number of self-help books on tape and began attending S.L.A.A. meetings.

At first I just sat in the back, whimpering while eating the free cookies.

"Hi, I'm X, and I'm a sex, love, fantasy addict!" one member quipped eagerly during the opening introductions.

"Hey, y'all, I'm Y—I'm a sexual anorexic!" another chimed with equal enthusiasm.

"Hi, I'm Lola, and I'm, um . . . just visiting."

The group's sympathetic gaze made me feel worse. I was a coward, and everybody knew it. The shortest of pauses convinced me I should provide more context.

"I mean, maybe I probably am a sex addict, but I don't really even have that much sex. Frankly, I would like to have *more sex*, at least more sex than my boyfriend does. So maybe that means I am a sex addict? And I was *raised* by other kinds of addicts, so there's probably something there?"

The women nodded kindly, which I misread as a sign to continue, despite one of them saying, "Gentle time."

"THE TRUTH IS," I pushed on, "I DON'T KNOW IF I BELONG HERE. HONESTLY, I THINK I'M JUST IN LOVE WITH SOMEONE I SHOULDN'T BE AND I CHEATED ON MY BOYFRIEND WITH HIM BUT NOT LIKE THAT BADLY. LIKE WE JUST MADE OUT AND SOME OTHER STUFF, WHICH IS NOT THAT BIG OF A DEAL. I THINK. I DON'T KNOW. MAYBE IT IS. I'VE NEVER CHEATED BEFORE. MY DAD CHEATED ON MY MOM A LOT, THOUGH, AND IT WAS *AWFUL*. BUT IF I JUST TELL YOU MORE ABOUT THE PERSON I CHEATED WITH MAYBE YOU'D UNDERSTAND BECAUSE HE HAS A REALLY DEEP VOICE AND STARCHES HIS JEANS 'CAUSE HE'S PRETTY MUCH A COWBOY. AND HE'S SO FUNNY AND SO KIND AND BASICALLY A MEMBER OF MENSA. LIKE HE'S *THAT* SMART. AND HE PLAYS GUITAR, WHICH KIND OF MAKES HIM SOUND LIKE A LOSER, BUT HE'S NOT 'CAUSE HE'S ACTU-ALLY GOOD AND I THINK HE JUST MOVED HERE 'CAUSE HE LOVES ME TOO. OR MAYBE HE MOVED HERE FOR WORK? I DON'T KNOW. BUT MAYBE

WE COULD ALL DISCUSS AND YOU COULD HELP ME DECIDE?"

A woman passed me a box of tissues. Apparently, I was weeping.

"Keep coming back," a few kind voices said before moving on.

After a couple weeks of rigorous attendance, I was getting good at "talking the talk" but struggling to "walk the walk," as they say. One day, I attended a meeting, as usual, braless and wearing a sheer skirt. After we said the closing Serenity Prayer, Lenora, the ballsy blond with thick glasses I'd asked to be my sponsor, an exciting step, I believed, laid out the rules: I wasn't allowed to talk to anyone I'd kissed, fucked, or flirted with, except Ian, for ninety days. I was also advised to reassess my wardrobe. This last part perplexed me. I was clearly the best dressed in the meeting. But I was "on my knees," as they say, and not in the fun way. So I listened to her.

When I looked in my closet later, I was mortified. I owned precisely three bras: one that I called my "audition bra," because it rounded my normally free-flying breasts into something more homogenous and TV-friendly. A second that came with a full bondage set and matching belly chain; and a third that I used for aerobics. How sick I was. I invested in some practical undergarments and began dressing like my memory of Deborah Kerr's chaste landscape painter

213

in *The Night of the Iguana.* I wore my hair in a very tight French braid that I complemented with a turtleneck, a large button-down shirt, and a larger sweater I'd wear over that. On my lower half, I wore wool tights, a maxi skirt, and tall boots.

In a way, it was a relief. I'd been outfitting my body to receive maximum attention for so long it hadn't even occurred to me that that was what I was doing. My whole life, I'd felt convinced beauty was a currency you had to spend to make more of. But I had been careless with it. Proving my worth to rude salesgirls in fancy shops, dropping it in fat stacks when I shouldn't. I was grateful to learn I could now hide it under the mattress. Even if I did look sort of Mormon.

I called a girlfriend to tell her about my progress. As the phone rang, I remembered how we'd made out once behind the port-a-potties at a wedding. Fuck. She was off-limits for the next ninety days. Thankfully, I'm popular. I hung up and dialed another pal.

"Erin!"

"Hey, girl, 'sup?" Erin replied, chipper as always.

"Oh, nothing! Actually, you know, never mind!" A memory of an eighth-grade game of spin the bottle with Erin was washing over me. I hung up.

Soon it became clear: there was no one I could talk to. Except Ian. I'd have to tell him.

At home, I found him on the porch, softly patting a small hand drum.

"Hi. Can you have an important conversation?" I asked, attempting to use some wise therapeutic language.

"Sure!" he replied nervously.

I told him the truth. Well, most of it. For a while he was just silent.

"You're really brave and strong, Lola," he said after a thoughtful pause. While there was a part of me that cringed at his constant use of words like "powerful" and "experience," another part of me had always appreciated his unflinching positivity.

"I've cheated on every girlfriend I've ever had, and I never had the guts to tell them about it," he continued.

"Wait, have you cheated on *me*?"

"No, I've never cheated on you," he said nobly, looking toward the sun. "I changed for you."

He began to cry.

"I'm so sorry, Ian," I kept saying.

"It's okay," he assured me through sobs. "Do you still wanna stay together?"

I thought about this for a minute. Having spent much of the week secretly attending S.L.A.A. and screaming in my car, I felt unmoored by his tenacious calm.

"I mean, if you do," I said, wishing it were true.

By day forty-seven of ninety, the Cowboy had texted precisely three times. The first was a sweet picture of an ugly dog named Merle. The second, an invitation to be his date to a fancy awards show. The third, an apropos-of-nothing review of an Atwater falafel restaurant he liked and a request to meet me there for lunch. I ignored them all.

After a while, the messages stopped. Ian and I started doing a lot better. We still weren't really having sex, but we were in couples therapy. We made charts about what made us feel fear and what made us feel safe. We hung them on the fridge so we could always be reminded.

When the Cowboy's birthday rolled around, I toyed with the idea of breaking the mandated ninety days of no contact to wish him a happy one. But Ian and I were planting an herb garden that day, and it crossed my mind that God might punish me for such a transgression by killing our basil. The Cowboy would probably think it was weird I remembered his birthday anyway. Though of course I did. I had to, in order to do our chart on a free astrology app.

A month later, I stopped going to S.L.A.A. altogether. A nineteen-year-old who couldn't stop getting circle-jerked on was making me feel out of place. Besides, I was pretty much cured. No longer did I spend my days driving past the house the Cowboy had mentioned living in. Just walking by on nights I got a little too drunk at a nearby friend's. They were practically neighbors!

That spring, I decided to check back in with my old S.L.A.A. meeting. I was sure they missed me. At the very least, my sense of humor and excellent style. Clad in a pair of patent-leather Mary Janes that would not disappoint and a prim-looking knee-length dress I hoped might convey my newfound sanity, I took my seat, all recovery and smiles. When sharing got underway, a young woman I'd been familiar with since my very first meeting raised her hand.

"Man, it's just crazy how high you can get as a sex and love addict without even trying!" she began.

Mmmm! I agreed.

"I was just down the street at that *falafel place*," she continued, as an image of the Cowboy popped into my head. He loved that place.

"When I ran into this guy I met at a party once years ago who was from *Texas*." Again, I thought of the Cowboy. He was from Texas. What synchronicity!

, "And I decided in that instant I was going to marry him."

Was it odd, or was it God? I'd had that very same feeling about the Cowboy when I'd met him. Was this my Cowboy? Or was this the problem with cowboys? They all liked falafel and made women fall instantly in love with them?

"And to make things worse, he told me he just moved here."

Finally, it hit me. This was no coincidence. It was the Cowboy. *My Cowboy.* I considered throwing the pot of free coffee at her, then screaming "HE'S MINE" very loudly, but reason told me that would be counted as cross talk. I left the meeting in a cold sweat. Maybe he wasn't my Cowboy after all.

That night, I made Ian go with me to a gay disco where I attempted to get a young starlet from a CBS All Access show to have a threesome with us and I don't even like those. She was offended. So was he. When I woke the next morning, Ian was very upset.

"I think you're unstable," he said solemnly.

I admitted I was and I thought we should separate, then took myself on a pilgrimage to the desert. It was the same trip I'd made often throughout my twenties, with many friends and much whiskey, hoping to catch a glimpse of Gram Parsons's ghost, staying in the motel room he'd lived and died in. Now, at twenty-nine, I was there alone, hoping to find only myself. After settling in, I stepped outside to smoke a cigarette. Grabbing the buckskin jacket I hadn't worn since Texas, I reached in its pocket for a light to discover the underwear I'd taken off at the bar all those months ago. I held them like a prayer in my hands, before wedging them inside a silly guitar-shaped shrine outside Gram's room. My time in twelve-step hadn't been entirely wasted. I knew now I could give things to God. I wondered what, if anything, I'd get back.

I found the Cowboy in Nashville a few months later. He kissed me against an abandoned church. After, on a dirt road under a full moon, I yelled that I loved him across a passed-out friend we were carrying home.

Right now, four years later, the sun is setting pink on the river that our house looks over. He'll be coming back from work soon. We'll eat dinner, talk about our days, then go to bed, our little dog rearranging himself over and over between us like a heat-seeking missile. I'm not that wild anymore. I have never felt so free.

CHARACTER ACTRESS

I wrote approximately a thousand and one songs about the Cowboy. Given the subject matter and my ever deepening love of the genre, they all came out country. Recording that many would take time, so after relocating to Nashville in 2020, I shifted my focus from acting to music. When the pandemic hit and movies stopped shooting, a more natural break was built in, and I was free to do as I pleased for a while. I never planned on quitting acting. Rather, I'd hoped to be a bit of everything, like Barbra Streisand, only with a worse voice and no *Yentl*. But when lockdown restrictions lessened and shooting picked back up, I was bereft to discover: acting may have quit me.

After nearly a decade of steadily working in film and TV, it seemed my luck had run dry. The series I'd spent years developing and finally sold to a major network was returned. A movie I was producing and starring in, and had finally secured financing for after three years, all but vanished. A fancy pilot I'd acted in as one of the leads didn't get picked up. Another movie I was cast in, which I didn't even really like but took anyway, hired me and then fired me a few weeks later because a more famous actress decided she wanted the part instead. A play I spent my life dreaming of doing, at a theater I'd dreamed of working in, cast me as one of the leads, then postponed the play three years, then canceled altogether a month before we were to start rehearsing.

To make matters worse: I turned *thirty*. Most of the time when you're an actress, this means you will start being considered for women of forty. For me, it meant ceasing to be considered for anything at all. Emi, meanwhile, never stopped working. To top it all off, my agents of over a decade dropped me in a two-and-a-half-minute phone call because of some merger or other. But not before my mother conspired with them, and my longtime manager, to get me on a diet, believing my size to be the culprit of my unemployability.

Despite having grown up in a very weight-conscious household and entering into an even more weight-conscious industry, I'd never actually been on a diet in my life. I didn't even have dietary *restrictions*. I ate whatever I wanted. Sure, a sound guy on my first movie had told me I was getting a "spare tire" from too much craft services. Sure, a costar once pinched my stomach between takes and told me I'd be prettier if I worked out more. But as excruciating as these experiences had been, they weren't real *thinspo*. Not even a costume designer accidentally sending a worried text *about* me *to* me instead of the director, saying I was "bigger than most actresses," could motivate me to lose weight. In fact, all that motivated me to do was reply to that sorry costumer saying I liked natural wine (I didn't really, I drank anything) and pink peonies, which I wished her luck finding (they were out of season). Both were in my trailer on the first day of filming.

Miraculously, I managed to like my body the way it was. When I discovered that my mother and my agents didn't, things shifted.

I first learned about their plot when the Cowboy confessed that my mom had also attempted to enlist him. He'd declined. I was shocked. Mostly because I hadn't noticed any changes in the first place. The Cowboy and I had spent the majority of lockdown in sweats at his place in Nashville. To glimpse my reflection in his only mirror, a small one for shaving that he'd hung to accommodate his six-four frame, I had to stand on my tippy-toes. Since that required a good deal of effort, whatever vanity I'd possessed was momentarily decimated. I stopped looking in the mirror long enough that I failed to notice I'd gained about twenty pounds. But when I learned everyone else *had* noticed, I was distraught.

I sobbed for a few days, then flew to New York to meet with Stacy. My manager since I was sixteen, Stacy was like a mother to me, taking me on even though I showed up to our first meeting in an oversize *Ren & Stimpy* T-shirt and jeggings—an act of magnanimity she likes to remind me of to this day.

At the Harvard Club (her alma mater, not mine), I hoped she wouldn't berate me about my body but apologize for ever having commented upon it. She didn't.

"Who says actresses have to be thin?" I sputtered.

"*Of course actresses don't have to be thin!*" she affirmed.

Sweet relief!

"But leading ladies do. Like this, you're more of a character actor."

For so long, I'd believed my body was no one else's business. The sad truth was my body was precisely Stacy's business. I left the Harvard Club feeling like a fool. I'd spent my life naively dreaming a career in film and TV would vindicate me from my family's trenchant beliefs about beauty and worth. The older I got, however, the clearer it became: my family's ideals just mimicked the very ones the industry itself espoused. It was a sick cycle, and only one thing would end it: dropping twenty. So I counted every calorie. I ran a half marathon. I even created my very own home workout video, à la Jane Fonda, set to an album of synth-driven '80s-inspired country music I'd made. I lost ten pounds. But I couldn't seem to lose any more. Nor gain any work.

Doing loops around the dog park in Nashville one afternoon some months later, I called Stacy and begged for answers.

"Actresses you're competing with work out six days a week!" she said.

"So do I!" I screamed, a golden retriever jogging to my side for emotional support.

"Well"—she paused dramatically—"I don't know what you eat."

My body flooded with shame. She was right. I still ate whatever the fuck I wanted. Just not as much of it, like my dieting app said.

In time I was able to get a few more jobs, with lower pay and in smaller parts. I was grateful, even when younger actresses on set asked me for directions like I was a crew member instead of a girl who had been in their very position only a few years earlier. My identity was changing and entering its awkward phase. Sometimes I lied when strangers asked what I did. I was an unmarried housewife. A doctor, but of poetry. Anything to avoid their condescending expressions when I said I was an actress: puzzled brows that seemed to say *I've never heard of you, so you're obviously not very good.* Smiles I knew well from years of smiling them myself, when I'd thought the exact same thing about someone else.

One evening the Cowboy and I were at a dingy Atlanta nightclub where he was scouting an act when a colleague of his scuttled over.

"So what do you do?" the record executive asked.

While I was sure he was just being polite, part of me suspected he shared in my existential confusion.

"Well," I began, "I make music."

"Ah," he said, as if saying goodbye.

"And I'm also an actress!"

He smiled an *oh-how-nice-for-you* smile.

"So do you do regional theater?" he asked.

"NO!" I yelled.

"Well what do you do, then?" he asked, concerned.

I began to stammer, wondering if, after all these years, there truly was an elegant way to list one's own IMDb credits. When I found myself crying them, I realized there wasn't.

"There's *nothing wrong* with regional theater," I said finally. "I just don't do it."

Back at the hotel later that night, the Cowboy tried to comfort me.

"I know how much your family makes you feel like you have to be *someone*," he said. "But sometimes I wish it was enough for you to be someone *to me*."

I wished it was too. But what I really wanted was for it to be enough for me to be someone to *me*.

Visiting my mother shortly thereafter, I decided to confront her about the weight-loss scheme.

"Mom," I began, "I would really appreciate it if, in the future, you didn't get involved in my work or ask my boyfriends to help you help me lose weight."

"I just—" She struggled to find the words. It felt like I was wounding a helpless animal. "I just want you to be *happy!*"

"Who says I'm not?"

"I only eat when I'm sad!" she declared.

"Well, we're different people," I said, trying to keep my cool. "And if you wanna know the truth, I actually mostly lose weight when I'm heartbroken. And I'm not right now. My life is *good*." And it was, except for this part of it.

"Okay," she said sadly. "Can I have a hug?"

As I considered my mom's request, I was reminded of a photo of her as a child. In it, she is round and unibrowed, a bewildered-looking toddler propped up next to her smiling blond mother. To scan the image once, I removed it from its frame only to discover it was actually a clipping from a newspaper. The caption, which had been obscured, read something like this: "Two-year-old girl left behind on a train. Hours later, her mother realized and came back to get her. Now they are reunited and couldn't be happier!"

I embraced her.

"I just know how important your work is to you," she said in my ear as I did.

It was important to me. I just wished it were less important to her.

Around this time, I got an exciting acting job in a TV adaptation of a book I'd loved that explored the sex lives of a few women and the bleak consequences of their desire. While I had originally auditioned for one of the three female leads, they ultimately offered me another role. Kelly was barely in the book itself, though they were beefing her up for the show. The one catch: she had to participate in a fifteen-page orgy sequence, which meant I would have to be fully nude save for the mandatory "merkin" (Hollywood for "pubic wig"). Determined to maintain my profile, lifestyle, and stance that my body was beautiful as it was, I took the job.

Since the role was small, there wasn't much to go off of. Still, I knew enough about acting to understand that even the most minor detail could reveal an entire character. Kelly was a florist. Kelly once wore a headdress to her Native American boyfriend's family powwow. Kelly liked magic mushrooms. Kelly wanted to have an orgy while on said magic mushrooms. Like a detective with a composite sketch, I was positive all this meant Kelly was very loud in bed and had a giant bush. When it came time to pick out Kelly's pubic wig, I told them to make it a big one, then headed off to rehearsal.

Since you typically don't rehearse for sex or TV, I wasn't sure what to expect. When I arrived at the soundstage, I was relieved to discover it was like any old play practice back in drama school. Actors were stretching each other in sweatpants, except these sweats were dry-clean-only. There were snacks. I was helping myself to a third free organic granola bar when the director emerged. She spoke in a soft accent as she explained her background was in mime, which would serve as the basis for our orgy work. Surreptitiously, I scanned the room to see if anyone else was as dubious as I. They weren't. A few moments later, the fifteen-page-orgy-people and I were silently exploring the *whole* space with our entire bodies, gently hitting each other's elbows with our palms, as we'd been taught, to "test each other's impulses."

After some of us broke down in tears, we were instructed to stop and introduced to a handsome woman named Myrtle. Myrtle was our intimacy coordinator, a relatively new position required on most sets in order to protect actors from unwanted intimacies. Since this scene saw me getting pounded from behind by a much older man before the much older man was scripted to *fart*, I was happy to take all the help I could get.

After the floaty mime stuff was through, we set about with the actual choreography.

"Thrust! Thrust! Thrust!" Myrtle clapped at my scene partner as I, the subject of the thrusts, lay obediently across a throw pillow.

"Now FART!"

The director made a fart sound with her mouth.

"Cue dialogue!"

We rehearsed the little sequence a few more times before nailing it (pun intended), then descended upon the soundstage beneath us. Built to resemble the interior of my character's greenhouse (remember: she was a florist), this was where the orgy was supposed to take place. I guess whoever wrote this script was unfamiliar with the old adage about wearing pants in a glass house. Anyway. After, we actors discussed dinner.

"I'm gonna do salmon again tonight," the other actress announced.

"I guess I will too," said one of the actors, his biceps rippling with each syllable.

"I'm just so bored of all this non-bloating food!" the third actor chimed in.

"Non-bloating food?" I asked, thinking all food was supposed to make you look like you were in your second trimester. The actors laughed in unison, flashing gorgeous white teeth. "How much of it do I need to eat to not be bloated?"

Suddenly, I was nervous.

"Don't worry, honey," the actress said. "You're beautiful just as you are."

And I believed her. Until I saw them all naked the next day. Their six-packs had six-packs. Even the men were hairless, a choice that made me almost regret the pubic wig I'd ordered, which spread from between my legs to just down the hall. As soon as I saw one of the men getting his abs sprayed to make them look somehow better, I asked if they might be able to do the same for me. There wasn't enough time, they said. It would take hours. Maybe everyone was right. I was too fat to be an actress. I shouldn't have taken the job. I panicked and ran to find the director.

"What if I stay clothed for the orgy?"

"Ah," she said, looking scared. "This is not possible—"

"Okay! Okay! How about, then, the straps of my dress come down so my boobs are out and the bottom of the dress comes up so you can see my butt but my stomach stays covered?"

She stared at me blankly.

"It will communicate the *passion* of the orgy. Like they just couldn't wait to get all her clothes off! They just had to start orgy-ing!"

She agreed it was a good idea. Though I was left to wonder what was so wrong with me that I was fine showing my tits and ass but would sooner die than show my stomach.

We shot my coverage first. I had my character hoot and holler the way I imagined a woman who mostly wore clogs would and I thought it went very well. But as soon as they started to film the other actors' close-ups, I began to regret my decision. Barely a whisper came out of their perfectly parted lips. It wasn't very real, but it looked *so much* better. Why did I always forget that part of acting?

At lunch, the other actress announced that she'd ordered an empanada truck for the crew. I was thrilled. Then I remembered I should restrain myself. I shouldn't gorge in front of my castmates—I shouldn't gorge at all. I shut myself into my dressing room instead.

I had wanted to be an actress my whole life. Initially because I wanted attention and later because I developed a deep love for the theater and cinema and the powers they possessed. When I was a teenager, my nightly ritual saw me curled up with a different movie and a box of LU Petit Écolier biscuits, doing my version of studying. I longed to be bawdy as Bette Davis, hoarse as Julie Christie, dynamic as Barbara Stanwyck, confounding as Shelley Duvall. No matter how glamorous they were, they were still odd enough to let me celebrate that same oddness in myself. They were aspirational and relatable. Perfectly imperfect, just as I hoped to one day be and help others feel. But after experiencing so much scrutiny around my body, all I felt was imperfect. I had grown to hate the way I looked on camera. I felt much more beautiful in real life. I wondered if I should finally quit acting after all.

When the break was over, I went back down to set to finish out the scene. As we waited to disrobe, I struck up a conversation with my costar, asking him how he'd spent lunch.

"Oh, ya know," he began, "just chatting with my daughter."

How strange, I thought. *This man has been pretend penetrating me for days now, and I didn't even know he had a daughter.*

"Is she an actress too?" I asked.

"No." He laughed. "Thank God."

For a long time, it seemed the show would never come out. As was now typical in my experience of Hollywood, the network folded and the one that bought it shelved it. The other day, I learned that the series had been quietly released in some tertiary markets via Instagram notification. A

South African fan account had set a clip of me on all fours to some strange tonal music. I slammed my phone down and screamed so loud my throat hurt. My hair looked terrible. They'd flat-ironed it.

There were a lot of things I wouldn't miss about acting. And a lot of things I would. Fortunately, I'd been writing a new character all my own: a country singer who wore rhinestones and glitter. Who could eat and drink whatever the fuck she wanted.

BROWNSTONE COWGIRL

If you ask me, I moved to Nashville by accident. If you ask the Cowboy, it was by force. We were just a few months into our relationship in February 2020 when he relocated there and rented a small back house. Being my mother's daughter and a member of a family I've heard described as "invasive," I took it upon myself to overhaul the design of its modest five hundred square feet. For my generosity, I expected nothing except his undying love and a nice place to stay when I visited him every other weekend from New York, where I'd just returned after my five-year stint in Los Angeles.

I made him buy plants even though he protested he'd forget to water them. Flatware. An expensive sofa he swore he'd never sit on.

"But where will you watch the curved flat-screen TV I just made you order?" I balked.

He shrugged, then pointed to one of the high-backed

oak chairs I'd picked out. They just went so perfectly with the nineteenth-century folding table I'd found.

"Don't be ridiculous," I said before asking for his billing zip to finalize the order on the Restoration Hardware website.

I had the kitchen walls painted Farrow & Ball's calm blue-gray, confoundingly named "Mizzle." The cabinets redone in black, replacing their thoughtless handles with some chic little midcentury ones I'd found online. Never mind that the room was so small you could hardly turn around in it. It was now a feat of design.

There was a new shower curtain. My favorite sheets and towels. Antique bamboo patio furniture. Turkish rugs. Everything was coming together when, about a month into my weekend excursions south, the news broke: a mysterious virus was raging. The whole country was forced into lockdown.

Perfect timing! I thought, even though the idea sounded a touch Soviet. I'd almost completed my decorating! All that remained was the delivery of a large Victorian mirror from Indiana.

"Thank God we got this couch," I said to the Cowboy that afternoon. We were sitting on it watching CNN.

"Oh," he said meekly. "You mean you're staying?"

My jaw fell slack. "Well, I hadn't planned to," I said, wondering if that was even true. Why else would I have convinced a man who couldn't boil water to purchase a Le Creuset cooking set in a gorgeous Mediterranean blue? "But if you send me home," I continued, "I could *die*."

Unfortunate footage of bodies being loaded into a U-Haul for proper storage, just a few neighborhoods north of mine in New York, flashed across the flat-screen.

"See?" I pleaded.

We skirted each other in the small but sweet two-room house for the next six months, mostly wearing matching sweatsuits we'd ordered in a shade of orange that made us look like prisoners. We fought. We laughed. I made pasta. Gained all that weight. The works—until I decided if we were going to live together, we may as well do it *properly*, and we bought a house.

And that's how I got to Nashville. I didn't hitchhike all night. I didn't hop a freight train. But I did spend a lot of my boyfriend's money on luxury home goods and make him feel responsible for my would-be death. Which really is another way of saying: *love* brought me here. And love certainly has its place in the pantheon of how guitar slingers, singers, dreamers, and the like find their way to Music City and get their start within it.

At least that's what I like to tell myself, every time I feel like a big, fat fraud for making country music. After all, country is American. Despite having lived in America for most of my life, I'm not. Not *really*—though I have tried to be American since I was a teenager, if only to distinguish myself from my English family.

Of course, individuating wasn't always the goal. When

I was much younger, I wanted nothing more than to bliss-fully fold into my mother and father and brother and sisters and even cousins, then all sleep in the same bed, like the grandparents in *Charlie and the Chocolate Factory*. I didn't care that nurturing my fading British accent did so little to promote my popularity among my American peers. Kids at school already found me snobby. I lived in a West Village brownstone and wore hand-me-down Vivienne Westwood, for god's sake. They were stuck in Old Navy, the poor things! I boasted about England like a gamer with a girlfriend in a foreign country. I ate Cadbury's exclusively. Celebrated all my birthdays at Tea & Sympathy, the West Village's leader in British cuisine, i.e., they dumped cans of Heinz baked beans, Heinz tomato soup, and Heinz sticky toffee pudding onto some darling mismatched tea plates, microwaved them, then sold it to you for the price of a ticket on the Concorde.

But when I saw how little my Britishness did to pro-mote the harmony I desired within my family, I decided to rebrand. By high school, I didn't want to fit in with them anymore anyway. It required standing out too much. There was so much sadness in our home. I longed to be a part of a happier one and set out to find it along the back roads of American music.

At first it was just Bob Dylan. Then Bob Dylan and the Band. Then just the Band. Their *Last Waltz* concert led me to Neil Young, who led to Buffalo Springfield, but also to

Crosby, Stills and Nash, which directed me to David Crosby's first band, the Byrds, in particular their album with Gram Parsons, *Sweetheart of the Rodeo*, which led to one bad tattoo I have since had covered, multiple "pilgrimages" to Joshua Tree, and country music as a whole.

Delving deeper into the genre, I rediscovered Patsy Cline (allegedly, when I was an infant, the only way to get me to stop crying was to have my baby nurse sing "Crazy" to me). Then I found Loretta and Tammy and Kitty. As an actress, I had always been drawn to dynamic female characters. In country, I found them. There, women could be complicated and contradictory. They could be mothers *and* lovers. Tough *and* tender. Glamorous *and* gritty, and all at once. Never mind the ever-present archetypal bleached teeth and hairpieces—the guys had them too! Not to mention, in country, men cried and apologized. For once.

Eventually, I was able to find some friends who shared my passion. My senior year of college—after Ada and I had called it quits—five of us started a short-lived all-girl country band, playing every Monday at the local bar. Unfortunately, that group came to an end when we realized our name was actually a racist slur in another language. We apologized to the offended community and disbanded. But my love of the genre remained. I discovered the outlaws. Waylon, Willie, etc. Later, I discovered what I like to call the in-laws (i.e., music your in-laws might enjoy): the Judds, Randy Travis, Vince Gill.

When I accidentally on purpose moved to Nashville, I

believed I had found my people. What I had failed to realize was that in the years that had passed since I fell in love with country, the music had changed a good deal. There were a lot more references to trucks, fishing, and trap music than I'd ever really gone in for. But a country song still told a complete story the listener could fully understand in just a few minutes. Having felt misunderstood my whole life, I wondered if country might hold my salvation.

Country music helped me make sense of the world, even if the country music I made seemed to make so little sense to the world. One esteemed publication that declared an album of '80s-inspired country disco I released a "pure delight" ultimately deemed it "egregious" (I had to look this up: it means "outstandingly bad"), as I wasn't Southern. A well-respected British publication said the album sounded like "a cheap home synthesizer being thrown down the stairs at Nashville Airport."

In any case, I got signed to an iconic Nashville label and toured, opening for seasoned female artists across the country spectrum. Some had their bands gather 'round as they read the Bible backstage before they played. Others had jars of many different strains of weed and mushrooms laid out in greenrooms for the taking. Some had both. Some were single and childless. Others piled their boyfriends and their babies on their buses, washing little socks and shirts in machines at the venue only to sell the place out a few hours later. Sometimes these women worried they should stay home more, not go out on the road so much. Others, they knew: without the road, they couldn't afford their homes. Not to mention, the road was their home.

As I watched these mothers, I couldn't help but think of my dad. Had he also been conflicted when he was on tour away from his young children? Or was that the bliss of being a man in music: the joy of fatherhood? You weren't responsible for it all. You weren't expected to be. The price of being a woman in music felt much higher. Did I want to pay it? How many other fees would I discover hidden in the small print?

One day, my record label sent me to a country songwriting conference hosted by a large music-streaming service. I knew I was in the right place from the huddle of men in pre-ripped jeans and trucker hats in the lobby. I knew the receptionist thought I was in the wrong place from the way she looked me up and down and asked, "Why are you here?" In truth, I didn't blame her. In a rumpled button-down shirt and below-the-knee skirt, I looked more like a tired Orthodox Jewish mother than an up-and-coming country artist.

Once inside, I took my place behind the spray-tanned back of the girl sitting in the chair in front of me, where I began to feel more out of place. Like most women in the room, she had gotten the cowgirl-hippie-dreamer memo that I hadn't. Unlike the other women in the room, however, she was wearing an engagement ring so big that when she raised her hand to ask a question, she had to use her other hand to assist it. A representative from the streaming service called on her.

"Caylin! Great to hear from you! What's your question?"

"My question is kinda two questions, except one isn't really a question," she drawled.

"Shoot," the streaming-service lady replied, oozing practiced corporate warmth.

"Okay, so, the first part is: I just love you guys so much." Caylin giggled nervously, as if she might cry. Her love was deep.

"And we love *you*!" the representative replied in a tone usually reserved for conversing with young children.

"And two is: I only have like twenty million streams on a song that just came out. Is that bad?"

The woman chuckled from the stage. I hung my head in shame. My last song had gotten something like twenty. "No, Caylin, that's very *good*! You're doing great!"

"Okay, that's what I thought! Thank you!"

No, thank you, *Caylin*, I thought to myself, *for making me feel terrible.*

The longer the conference continued, the worse I felt. For so long, my fantasy of America had been the solution to my English alienation. Now the reality of American culture was beginning to make me feel alone all over again. In the elevator after, I wondered at the connection between my two passports and my two professions. Had I just run to Nashville because I didn't know where I'd fit in Hollywood, the way I'd once tried to be American after giving up trying to be British? Where would I run to next? Who was I kidding that I was a country singer, anyway? I had been desperate to escape the one farm I'd ever spent time on *and* I was currently wearing loafers!

"Who's your artist?" a woman riding down with me asked, jolting me out of my self-doubt spiral. She was sporting a Bluetooth headset circa 2006, sucking from a straw attached to a gallon of water with a handle like a handbag.

"Excuse me?" I replied, not catching her meaning.

"Who do you manage? You're a manager, right?" she said, her eyes trained on my Tod's.

I supposed this was a step up from when I'd recently been asked if I was a "seat filler" at a Nashville awards show. I was about to correct her when it occurred to me I actually didn't know what I was anymore either. Was I a musician? An actress? English? American? Heavier than I'd like? Totally happy in my body? A fucking mess? Just plain human?

"I'm a country singer," I said finally.

From what I knew of country music and complicated women, I understood the rest might be implied.

"Well, I like your look." She smiled between slurps. "Very unique!"

The doors opened. She clacked her direction in little

clacky sandals. I went mine. By the time I reached my truck, the one with the Dolly plates that I'd bought to blend in better in Tennessee, I was beginning to think maybe being unique wasn't such a bad thing. If growing up as I did taught me anything, it's that sometimes the best way to fit in is by standing out.

MY OPRY DEBUT

I am backstage at the Grand Ole Opry, wearing June Carter's dress. I am backstage at the Grand Ole Opry, America's most beloved and oldest radio show, about to sing songs I wrote, in front of thousands of people, wearing June Carter's dress. I am backstage at the Grand. Ole. Opry: the home of country music, about to make my Opry debut, and I am wearing. June. Fucking. Carter's. Perfect. Dress.

These were the words going through my head as I was finally breaking from reality.

Just kidding! These were the words going through my head as I was, you guessed it—backstage at the Opry, about to make my Opry debut (and I'll say this once more for effect: wearing June Carter's dress). Having been lucky enough to have a few dreams come true, I'd learned well how anticipating one can eclipse the actual experience. It's always been easier for me to look forward than look around. But I didn't want to let this dream go down the same way. I wanted to stay present for it. This dream was unique. This dream was all mine.

While I was raised to believe I could (and *should*) become some kind of artist, I was never raised to believe I could (and should) become a *country* artist. While country music had been an oddly large part of my cosmopolitan existence since I was a teenager, initially, it was only a part of my private life: a world I could run toward, two steps at a time, up to my room and away from whatever chaos was happening downstairs. It lived in records I'd play so loud that I almost couldn't hear my parents screaming at each other. It lived in the voices of long-dead cowboys I loved and saw on the backs of those records. In songs I tried to learn on my ukulele, which annoyed everyone, or on my banjo, which annoyed everyone more.

Country music wasn't just an escape from my life but a key to understanding it. Cheating songs like "After the Fire Is Gone" helped me empathize with my father's pain. "Stand by Your Man," my mother's loyalty. In country, the most complicated feelings were rendered perfectly simple. Since my family had a knack for making the simplest things as difficult as, say, performing open-heart surgery if you are an orangutan, in country I saw a solution: start a family band and tour extensively. But that was never going to happen. We'd all want to sing lead. So throughout my teens, country remained to me what New York City is to a lot of people: a world that I fantasized would accept and understand me better than my own, if only I could get there. I had no way of knowing then that, within two decades, I'd be living in the country-music capital of the world, tirelessly repeating: *I am backstage at the Opry, wearing June Carter's dress.*

Staying awake for my dream wasn't the only reason for that mantra. I was also hoping to avoid a nightmare that had been unfolding over the past—well, six or so generations of my family, really, but for the sake of brevity—few months.

It all started around the time I got invited to play the Opry. Naturally, I took this as a cue to invite everyone I had ever met, including a bus driver I'd once hit it off with and my entire family. Ever since leaving home at seventeen, first for college, then California, now Tennessee, I'd longed to have my family step into my world and say: *Wow! Look at how organized your cabinets are! You're perfect! We're sorry!* Then turn around and leave. By "my family," I really mean my siblings. And by "my siblings," I really mean my sisters. Sorry, G, it's a girl thing.

My sisters are about six and eight years older than me, respectively. They both had kids when they were very young, which means they have been mothers for the entirety of my adult life and the majority of theirs. This has necessitated that our grown-up relationships be cultivated in stolen moments. There is no time for girls' trips. Nights out are rare, if ever. I have come to take for granted that plans are canceled, texts unanswered. After all, motherhood is demanding and unpredictable. But the truth is I've never felt my sisters were available to me. Accessing them has always required stepping into their world. I yearned for them to take an interest in mine. I hoped my Opry debut would be the thing to finally get it.

To my surprise, both sisters accepted the invitation. In fact, everyone in my family did. Well, everyone except my dad, who would be celebrating his seventh wedding anniversary in Europe during that time.

"I thought you got married in the summer?" I said, hoping he could squeeze in my February debut. Though I hadn't been to either of his two weddings to his new wife (one at a friend's oceanfront estate in the Hamptons, another in an English castle), a photo of my stepmother at the altar in angel wings was burned into my brain. As I recalled, it looked quite warm out.

"No, we did a court wedding too," he corrected, adding a third to the list. "If you've ever given up on love: just go to city hall on Valentine's Day!"

As the date got nearer, I was shocked to discover that no one else in my family was even canceling, a fact so astonishing I had to confirm it via text at least a few times a week. Soon my dad even wrote to tell me that his trip had fallen through, so they'd make it after all. As the day grew closer, I felt consumed by guilt. I was making too much of myself. Sure, this was a big deal, but not for someone like me, who'd probably only gotten this opportunity because I was relatively well behaved, moderately talented, and in close enough proximity to those that people actually cared about.

Plus, in keeping with the format of the show, I'd only be singing two songs. It was a long way to make people travel for just two songs.

When the week before the Opry they all maintained they were still coming, I began to grow wary in a new way. If they all showed up, I would have to rewrite my lifelong narrative that they never did. That sounded exhausting! But also exciting. What would it be like to have a family I could trust to just be there?

A few days before, Mino called.

"How do you feel?" she said, a smile in her voice.

"Good!" I answered. "Also scared! Like the other shoe is gonna drop at any moment!"

"*Well*," she replied, her tone shifting now to the familiar one that meant she was about to let me down. "The only shoe that *might* drop is that we've all been sick for ten days."

I thought back to myself in college, when, after I'd skipped the lion's share of an eight a.m. Contact Improv class, somehow a graduation requirement, the professor failed me. I gave her lots of excuses. Illnesses, deaths. A hurricane. While I omitted some hangovers, I was mostly telling the truth.

"I'm so sorry, Lola, that really does sound like a lot." She smiled sadly. "But it doesn't change the fact that you still don't know the basic principles of contact improvisation. Like spiraling."

I tried to explain that she was wrong: a fundamental of

the form, spiraling looked and felt just like scissoring, only with your clothes on.

"You just haven't been here," she replied warmly. "I can't pass you."

On the phone with my sister, I considered telling her the same thing: *I don't care how legitimate your reasons are. You don't show up. You are failing.* Instead, I wished her a speedy recovery. She canceled the next day.

As the week rolled on, friends of mine poured into town from all over: Los Angeles. New York. Red Cloud, Nebraska.

"Friends are God's apology for your family," my mother had told me when I was much younger. I had quite a few by now. I wondered if this meant He was really sorry.

Even Rose surprised me two days prior to the main event, on Valentine's Day, all the way from Wales. I felt grateful to be so loved. But again, I felt guilty. I knew my sisters didn't have friendships like I did. At least I knew Emi didn't.

"How many friends do you have?" she asked me on the phone the day before the big show.

I counted the gorgeous women gathered in my living room, stretching responsibly before a workout class I'd organized for us. "Five!"

"You have *five friends*?" She sounded shocked.

"I mean I have five friends over *right now*," I said. "Oh! And one still sleeping downstairs."

"Wow," she replied, sounding at once impressed and depressed.

"They can be *your* friends too, once you're here!" I blurted, trying to entice her not to cancel while also wondering if that was even true.

Over the past few years, my tough big sister had grown dizzyingly frail. The ice around her heart had finally thawed, but too much, like someone had thrown it in the microwave on the wrong setting. Liquid now, it dripped between your fingers when you tried to put it back together.

I feared her fragility would be just as formidable to my adult friends as her cruelty once was to my childhood ones. Then I reassured myself it wasn't. Everyone loved Emi. They always would.

That night as I was falling asleep, I got a text from my mom: "How do I get tickets?"

"With the link," I shot back angrily. "I sent it three months ago."

"But where do I sit? I need ten tickets!"

My anger was overcome by my guilt. *I should help my mother*, I thought. *She's just trying her best to be there for me. But I already did*, I reminded myself. *And right now, her best is very annoying.* I sent the link over again anyway but ignored her follow-up text, where she asked how to open it.

The next morning, my mother called.

"MY FLIGHT HAS BEEN CANCELED!" She was sobbing at the airport, as was her habit. "What do I do?"

"Where are you?" I replied, unsure which of her many residences she was in.

"New Orleans," she wailed.

"Well." I breathed deep. "You could start driving *now* and be here in eight hours if you don't stop. Or you could book another flight."

"But what *should* I do?" she begged.

"I trust that whatever decision you make is gonna be the right one," I said before telling her I loved her and hanging up.

The rest of the day was a breeze. Some of the girls and I got gel mani-pedis and lounged around. Then a few of them drove me in my Dolly truck to the Opry. We screamed when we saw my picture on the marquee outside. When a security guard directed us to a parking spot designated *just for me* with my very own plaque, we screamed again. They watched like loving parents as I carried my guitar case through the storied artists' entrance for the first time—a once in a lifetime experience, never to be repeated. Until a few moments later. A camera crew was on hand to document the entire event for a special segment called *My Opry Debut* and they needed that shot.

"And action!" the director cried, as I looked up at the

red awning the very way I had five minutes earlier, smiling widely.

"Maybe say something happy?" he suggested.

"I'm just so . . . happy!" I fumbled. My worst performance to date. Playing yourself, it turns out, is very hard. Fortunately, I'd have time to perfect it. The cameras would stay with me for the rest of the evening, with the exception of when I changed.

At sound check, I stepped into the circle—the original Opry floorboard from way back when—for the very first time. I sang with the twelve-piece house band to an empty auditorium, imagining how, in a few short hours, it would be filled with strangers and friends and family, seeing me as I'd always wanted to be: center stage with my guitar, and some fake hair clipped onto my head.

Afterward, things went into high gear. There was makeup to do. Interviews to give. Social media plugs to film. Showtime was close upon us when I heard a familiar voice: "Hi, my favorite."

In my dressing room mirror, I saw Lilith, standing in the doorway. A few years after my brother had passed away, she'd returned to Nashville, where she'd had a successful career managing country artists in the '90s. Sometimes I wondered at this synchronicity. Perhaps my little brother had brought me to the place he was born, to start this new chapter of my life. Gratefully, I'd tried to maintain a relationship, but without my brother there to bind us, ours began to feel the same as others within my family: as if I owed her something I could never give enough of.

Management interrupted with a ten-minute warning.

"I thought the show started at seven thirty?" I panicked, as that was what I'd told everybody.

"No, *you* go on at seven thirty. The *show* starts at seven."

Reason told me this would make no difference: if my family believed the show started at seven thirty, and I went on at seven thirty, they'd be right on time for my set! Plus they all had tickets that said the time of the show on them, and they would look at those . . . right? Instead of relying on me? *Right?*

Frantically, I sent a group text to everyone I'd ever met. A few people wrote back that they were already in their seats, including G, who sent a few photographs of my happy nephews eating some popcorn and giving a thumbs-up. God love G.

Other texts weren't so comforting.

Mum: WE ARE IN TRAFFIC I AM DOING EVERYTHING

Emi: Mum said the show was at 7:20? I am still at hotel.

I was attempting to untangle Emi's logic *(You thought the show started earlier and you're still not here?)* when my phone began to ring. It was my dad.

"Hey, love," he said, sounding chipper as ever, "we're having a hard time getting into the building—could you send someone to come get us and bring us backstage?"

My blood could have boiled an egg. Then I thought

about him boiling me eggs when I was a child, which made me soften ever so slightly.

"The show has already started and I'm about to go on," I said, attempting calm. "I'd love it if you could just go to your seats."

It was no use. Within moments, he and my stepmother were in my dressing room. Fortunately, Lilith had just left.

"Monkey!" he said with spirit-crushing pep.

"Dad, *please* go sit in the audience," I begged while trying to sound as happy as possible. After all, the cameras were still rolling. Ignoring my plea, he leaped in front of my dressing room piano and began to plunk out what can only be described as . . . *the boogie-woogie.* A lovely moment for the segment. I would have cried if not for how soon I was going to be in front of *even more* cameras and on a Jumbotron. Not to mention how good my blue eye shadow looked.

Side stage, I waited with my guitar in the dark. June Carter's dress clung to my body like a gold-sequined hug. I had ten minutes out there. I resolved I wouldn't let anyone ruin a single second of it.

"She was born in London," the host began, "and raised in New York City. Not only is she a great singer-songwriter, but she's an incredible actress as well."

Having felt so complicated my whole life, I was struck by how simple I sounded when the world's oldest country-music radio show described me. Maybe I wasn't so complicated after all. Or maybe that was just the great power of country music: the complicated can become gorgeously simple.

"Tonight she is making her Grand Ole Opry debut," the emcee continued. "Please welcome Lola Kirke!"

I made my way across the stage and into the circle.

"Hey, y'all," I said, employing the South's signature contraction. It was, after all, the Opry.

I sang and played well. Between songs, I made a successful joke. I started a clap for the first time in my career too, a bold move I wasn't sure I was capable of pulling off, but I had shaved my armpits for just in case. Not even seeing my mother jostle into the auditorium in the middle of my first song could sway me. I was just happy she'd made it. She always did. Just in her own way. She looked proud as she pushed her way to the front.

After I hit my last note, I curtsied twice, then walked over to the host for the post-show interview.

"How did it feel?" he asked.

I replied I was just relieved my hairpiece did not fall out. The crowd laughed.

"I have an important question for you, Lola," he continued. "Will you join us again?"

It felt like I'd finally found the American home I'd set out in search of all those years ago. Though of course I would be leaving as soon as they needed me to clear out of the dressing room. My mother had taught me never to overstay my welcome.

Backstage, I was drinking a celebratory plastic cup of warm champagne when Lilith returned. As soon as she did, my phone rang. It was my dad: "Can you send someone back out to get us?"

Hoping to avoid a reunion in my dressing room between my father and a woman he'd sired a child with, I tried to explain that things were a little chaotic. Maybe I could just see him tomorrow? The cameras were still rolling. Something that soap operatic would be a bit dramatic for such a short segment.

But a few moments later, there he was, a genuine smile of fatherly pride in his eyes. He pulled me in for a tight hug. I allowed myself to briefly revel in his embrace before breaking the news.

"Lilith's here," I whispered apologetically in his ear.

"What?" he replied.

The color drained from his cheeks as he looked up to see her across the room. She smiled as she floated toward him. I averted my gaze. Stealing a glance shortly after, I noticed her holding his face in her hands. She still loved him after everything that had happened. We all did.

We took more photos. I met more people—country legends of all stripes, other guests on the show that night.

When it came time to go, I shed June's dress like armor I no longer needed. Back in my blue jeans, I met my friends at the Nashville Palace, a bar almost as legendary as the Opry itself, just down the road. I had hoped Emi would come too, that she could take another step into my world while she was in it, but traveling alone with the kids had been exhausting, she said. They needed rest. I felt sad, but I was glad at least she'd made it, and sent her a text saying so.

"You were perfect, Lola," she replied. "You won."

After years of feeling like a loser around my sister, I would have expected hearing that I'd won would make me feel vindicated and provide the affirmation I'd longed for. When I read her message, however, it just stung. I didn't want to win. I didn't want to be ahead of her. Nor did I want to be behind her either. I wanted to be with her. With all of them. Now here they almost all were, in Nashville, and I was with none of them. The evening had been a success—the type I'd long fantasized would bring my family together and win me the love I'd craved. But in that moment I began to see: success was just success. It was not the key to love. It was a distraction from it. I had all my family's love already. Our love just looked a little different than I thought it should.

A band was playing at the bar. During a break in their set, the singer came around to our table with a bucket for tips.

"She just made her Opry debut!" my friends screamed in her direction.

258

"Well, then you'll have to come sing with us onstage! It's a tradition! What songs do you know?"

"Uh—" I stammered.

"Do you know any Patsy Cline?"

"Yes!" I yelled.

"How about 'Crazy'?" the singer suggested.

I considered it. It was the first song that had ever been sung to me by my baby nurse. The first song I ever learned to play on the ukulele. The first song I sang at karaoke with the Cowboy, to win him over. But I wasn't a baby anymore. I hadn't played the ukulele in years. And I'd won the Cowboy over long ago. It was time to move on. I didn't want to be crazy anymore anyway.

"How 'bout 'Walkin' After Midnight'?" I said.

Rock and roll, country's wild kin, is at its best when it is rebelling. When it gyrates and burns guitars and bites the heads off winged creatures. When it breaks the rules. Country, on the other hand, is all about following them. First there are the rules you must obey to achieve its form—its signature chord progression, the 1-4-5. More importantly, there are the rules within its songs that you hear their singers chafe against. Anthems of women struggling to be good mothers in spite of everything. Ballads of men repentant that they weren't better husbands in spite of themselves. Songs about hearts and traditions that had to be broken. Highways you had to travel away from houses that built you. Tropes like these are what make the genre appealing to so many. It is luxurious to buck the system. It is far more universal to long to work within it.

While there are no dirt roads and there's certainly more than one stoplight, when I hear songs like that, I can't help but think of New York City. The homes I lived in. The characters I grew up around. The tight spaces I tried and often failed to wedge myself into. The dent they all left on my heart that I no longer mind having. What better way to be reminded it has been so well loved?

The Cowboy often points out the New York in me. When we are at the grocery store and, instead of making polite small talk, I am buying things on my phone, frustrated the cashier is taking so long. When I swear it takes twenty minutes to get anywhere and I am at least twenty minutes late for everywhere. When I cry in public. Try as I might to change, I am learning to accept that I'll probably always be the same: a little different. A lot more like my family than I even realized. Like the West Village, Manhattan's only neighborhood that diverges entirely from its otherwise perfect grid, we are each a mess of chaos and idiosyncrasies. Sometimes it's charming. Sometimes you get very lost. But sometimes you need to get lost to find your own way.

ACKNOWLEDGMENTS

This book would not be possible without the influence of the most dazzling characters I have ever known. My father, Simon. My brother, Greg. My mother, Lorraine, and of course, my sisters, Domino and Jemima. I spent my life hoping to follow you both down the creative trails you blazed and be an artist. Throughout the process of sharing my work with the world, you assured me I was one. I am so excited for the new stories we will write together. I cannot wait to read your books . . . Or can I?

Next, I'd like to acknowledge my longtime "momager" Heather Reynolds. My kind and wonderful literary agent, Leah Petrakis, who was impulsive enough to ask if I "had a book" in me. Carina Guiterman, my long-suffering and hilarious editor and her team at Simon & Schuster. Rhonda Price at Gersh. Marla Farrell and Jessica Sze at Shelter PR. Hildy Gottlieb, Bonnie Bernstein, and Dan Kirschen at CAA.

My friends who not only tolerated my reading them drafts of these stories aloud but requested that I do: Marianne Rendon, Cornelia Livingston, Greta Morgan, Courtney Marie Andrews, Lilah Larson.

Others who helped shape my work in various ways: Elizabeth Sonenberg, Charlotte Benbeniste, Rachel Libeskind, Danielle Aykroyd, Lana Barkin, Chelsea Crowell, Jordan Williams, Hailey Benton-Gates, Vesta Fort. Hannah, Audrey. Alex O Eaton, for sending out writing prompts during the pandemic that sparked me, Jenny Lewis whose kitchen table in Nashville provided a room of my own where I first started writing these pages . . . Gael. Wyndham. Jack. Charlie. Gus. Linda. Gaby. Olive May. Marissa and Simon. Pamela Hanson.

The writers I admire who assured me I wasn't bad and should keep going: Emma Forrest, whose work and mind I've loved as long as I've known her. David Adjmi. Rosanne Cash. Thank you.

Lastly: Austin and Santino, my little wolf pack. I love you more than my words could ever say. Thank you for holding me and sitting on my lap respectively throughout the whole ordeal of writing this not memoir.

ABOUT THE AUTHOR

Lola Kirke is an acclaimed actress and singer-songwriter. *Wild West Village* is her first book.